IMAGES OF WAR

I0884593

UNITED STATES ARMY ARMORED DIVISIONS OF THE SECOND WORLD WAR

RARE PHOTOGRAPHS FROM WARTIME ARCHIVES

Michael Green

Pen & Sword
MILITARY

First published in Great Britain in 2019 by
PEN & SWORD MILITARY
An imprint of
Pen & Sword Books Ltd
47 Church Street
Barnsley
South Yorkshire
S70 2AS

ISBN 978-1-52671-752-2

A CIP catalogue record for this book is available from the British Library.

Typeset by Concept, Huddersfield, West Yorkshire HD4 5JL.
Printed and bound in India by Replika Press Pvt. Ltd.

Pen & Sword Books Limited incorporates the imprints of Atlas, Archaeology, Aviation, Discovery, Family History, Fiction, History, Maritime, Military, Military Classics, Politics, Select, Transport, True Crime, Air World, Frontline Publishing, Leo Cooper, Remember When, Seaforth Publishing, The Praetorian Press, Wharncliffe Local History, Wharncliffe Transport, Wharncliffe True Crime and White Owl.

For a complete list of Pen & Sword titles please contact
PEN & SWORD BOOKS LIMITED
47 Church Street, Barnsley, South Yorkshire S70 2AS, England
E-mail: enquiries@pen-and-sword.co.uk
Website: www.pen-and-sword.co.uk

Contents

Dedication

This book is dedicated to Philip M. Cavanaugh,
former director of the Patton Museum of Cavalry and Armor.

Foreword

Historians, armchair generals and pundits have on the one hand welcomed the invention of the tank in warfare and then, upon the end of the current conflict, raised the death knell of armoured warfare in future conflicts. An exception to this was the Second World War. The tank was evaluated and upgraded; lessons learned were implemented; training programmes, doctrine, tactics, techniques and procedures were evaluated, torn apart and rewritten.

This is where *United States Army Armored Divisions of the Second World War* and its author fit into the historical literature of the Second World War. It is a brilliant, condensed overview of the struggle, the promise and the performance of the armoured forces and their leaders in the Second World War. From an almost infantile beginning during the First World War at the nadir of strategic and operational thought to abandonment during the interwar period during the Great Depression, armoured forces saw their rise and explosion into operational warfare during the Second World War.

Randy R. Talbot
Command Historian (retired)
US Army TACOM Life Cycle Management Command

Acknowledgements

The historical images in this work come from a variety of sources including the files of the now closed Patton Museum of Cavalry and Armor, the TACOM Historical Office and The National Archives. For the sake of brevity, images from the Patton Museum of Cavalry and Armor will be credited to the Patton Museum. Those individuals who kindly supplied images are credited within the captions.

Chapter One

The Beginning

By 1915, the French and British armies were stalemated by trench warfare. The Germans, protected by extensive trench systems and machine guns with interlocking fields of fire and artillery, were almost impossible to dislodge from their defensive positions. Thus the tank, developed in great secrecy, was first fielded by the British Army in 1916 and by the French the next year. Results were less than impressive for a variety of reasons such as inadequate numbers, lack of a well-thought-out doctrine on how they were to be employed, and their poor mechanical reliability.

Following America's entry into the war, the US Army formed the 'Tank Board' in July 1917. Tasked with reviewing their allies' experience, the board was to recommend US Army organization and doctrine for the use of tanks. Two months later, the board recommended that the army establish a separate tank arm within the American Expeditionary Force (AEF). General John J. Pershing, commander of the AEF, authorized the forming of the Tank Corps in December 1917. He placed Colonel Samuel D. Rockenbach, a former cavalry officer like himself, in charge of the new organization.

Issues Confronting the Tank Corps

For a variety of reasons including bureaucratic incompetence, ineptitude and malfeasance within American industry and the US Army leadership concerned with weapons development, no American-designed and built tanks would see combat during the First World War. This would force the Tank Corps to depend on both the British and French armies for the vehicles they required. As the former was not convinced that the Tank Corps would make productive use of their tanks, few were provided. The French Army, on the other hand, proved to be a more dependable supplier of tanks.

With no practical experience in the employment of tanks, the brand-new Tank Corps was forced to seek assistance from the British and French armies which had conflicting doctrines reflected in their tank designs. British doctrine specified that tanks would lead the way, breaking through German defences with their fire while protecting the crews. British infantry would follow, 'mopping up'. British tanks were therefore heavy and heavily-armoured, moving no faster than the pace of a walking soldier.

French doctrine espoused the concept of light tanks accompanied by infantry breaking through enemy lines together, with heavy tanks (in reality self-propelled artillery pieces) providing fire support from the rear: a combined-arms approach. Colonel Rockenbach decided that the Tank Corps would integrate elements of both allies' tank warfare doctrine, with heavy tanks breaking through enemy lines on their own, followed by infantry accompanied by light tanks.

Incorporating both of these doctrines into the Tank Corps meant that separate training schools had to be established respectively under British and French guidance. Those serving in heavy tanks went to a training camp in Great Britain, while those who were assigned to light tanks went to a training camp in France. The commander of the latter training camp was George S. Patton Jr, a cavalry officer who had been through the French Army light tank school only a short time before. Patton had been selected for the task by General Pershing, commander of the AEF, as he spoke fluent French.

French tank warfare doctrine proved to have the most influence over Tank Corps leadership in formulating an American organization and doctrine. This can be attributed to its close proximity to the front lines and the combat experience and lessons learned provided by French tankers coming directly off the battlefield. The tank training school in Great Britain lacked access to this type of rapid battlefield feedback.

Into Battle

The Tank Corps committed two newly-formed light tank battalions to the Battle of St. Mihiel, which began on 12 September 1918. The two battalions, under the command of the US 304th Brigade commanded by Patton, fielded 144 French light tanks. Results were not as impressive as hoped for as the tanks were slow, short-ranged and mechanically unreliable, reflecting the capabilities of current components, manufacturing, materials and engineering. All this was made much worse by the muddy conditions of the Western Front.

Patton had tried to overcome the anticipated obstacles posed by the existing tank designs and the terrain on which they were to fight by inspiring his men with his own aggressive attitude. One of Patton's junior officers recounted that Patton's favourite messages to his officers went something like this: 'Go forward, go forward. If your tank breaks down, go forward with the infantry. There will be no excuse for your failure in this, and if I find any tank officer behind the front lines, I will probably shoot him.' The same officer recounted that Patton made him understand that a tank officer was meant to die!!!

Of the 144 light tanks committed to the Battle of St. Mihiel, only three were knocked out by enemy fire, while another forty were lost to mechanical failure or immobilized on the battlefield by terrain features. From a transcript in the files of the Patton Museum of Armor and Cavalry comes this brief passage by US Army AEF Tank Corps Lieutenant Harold H. Neff who participated in the Battle of St. Mihiel:

> The first day of the attack, my company was supposed to be in reserve. After the attack had been well started, we crept along, over trenches, far away. The column stopped, as the leading elements were having great difficulty with a wide and deep trench. Suddenly, in the quietness that there was, crash went a shell right over there. We decided that it was best to scatter helter-skelter until a crossing could be negotiated. Machine-gun bullets started singing quite a bit. Under the calm supervision of Colonel Patton, after several tanks had unsuccessfully attempted to cross and were ditched in the mire, the 1st Platoon of my company succeeded in passing and was sent up the hill to get 'those machine-gun nests'.

The French Army quickly replaced the three tanks destroyed by the enemy at the Battle of St. Mihiel. On 26 September 1918, the Meuse-Argonne Offensive began with the Tank Corps playing a small part. By the time the war concluded with the signing of the Armistice on 11 November 1918, the Tank Corps was down to approximately fifty operational light tanks.

Patton's desire to lead from the front in that second operation almost cost him his life when he was badly wounded by German machine-gun fire. Rockenbach (promoted to brigadier general) was not impressed by Patton's zeal in wanting to lead from the front and had in no uncertain terms warned him after the Battle of St. Mihiel that as a brigade commander he needed to be at his command post at all times. In addition, he informed Patton that he appreciated the fighting spirit he had created among his men and the resulting acts of personal valour by many of them. In future, all were to be advised 'that they are fighting [in] tanks, they are not infantry, and any man who abandons his tank will in the future be tried [by court-martial].'

The only other Tank Corps operation of the First World War involved the 301st Heavy Tank Battalion, which was under British Army command. It played a small part in an allied offensive operation referred to as the Battles for the Hindenburg Line, which ran from 12 September 1918 until 12 October 1918. From the files of the Patton Museum of Armor and Cavalry comes this brief passage by US Army Tank Corps Sergeant Carl E. Rosenhagen on what happened to his tank:

> Then a shell hit us on the right side and tore a hole in our back end, busting our main water line running up to the motor. In no time, steam filled the tank so bad that I don't know how any of the rear crew lived through it, as we had our front

> windows open gasping for air ... There were two terrific explosions outside of the tank, and then a shell hit us on top. I believe the motor casing saved us. We heard a big plop inside and we caught on fire; the whole tank seemed on fire. I climbed through Lieutenant Dunning's seat, the only way I could get out and came along the motor by the six-pounder [57mm gun] over the transmission when I saw the lower door open on the right side, and I slid out.

Of approximately thirty British-supplied heavy tanks, only eleven of the 301st Tanks reached their assigned objective during the fighting. The remaining vehicles were either destroyed by enemy action or lost to mechanical issues or terrain obstacles on the battlefield.

By the time the Germans signed the Armistice on 11 November 1918, the Tank Corps consisted of some 12,000 men. There were another 8,000 men being trained in the United States for deployment as tankers in France. In the United States, all tanks and those training to serve overseas in the tanks of the Tank Corps belonged to what was originally referred to as the 'Tank Service', later renamed the Tank Corps, which was a separate entity from the Tank Corps that had formed part of the AEF in France.

The largest training camp in the United States for tankers heading overseas was commanded by Captain Dwight D. Eisenhower from the infantry branch. Captain Eisenhower preferred to serve in combat with the Tank Corps, but the approval for his overseas transfer came too late, so much to his dismay he missed seeing action in the First World War.

Post-War Re-Think on Tanks

With the end of the First World War, commonly referred to as 'the war to end all wars', the American Congress began a massive post-war demobilization of the US Army. By March 1919, the Tank Corps had returned to the United States with some of its French and British tanks but was down to approximately 3,300 men. It was at this same time that production of an American-modified version of a French light tank design and an American/British co-production heavy tank, both initiated in 1917, finally began rolling off the assembly lines in numbers.

On Rockenbach and Patton's return to Fort Meade, Maryland in 1919, they were joined by Eisenhower. Patton and Eisenhower then began putting on paper some of their thoughts on the importance of expanding the Tank Corps and its potential future. All this would prove to be for nought as the American Congress decided to dissolve the independent Tank Corps and the supporting Tank Board under the 4 June 1920 National Defense Act. From that moment on, tanks were placed under the command of the newly-created 'Chief of Infantry' and employed only in the infantry support role.

Congress was heavily influenced in the decision to abolish the independent Tank Corps by an appearance before them the year before by Pershing, then chief of staff of the US Army, and his aide Colonel George C. Marshall, Jr from the infantry branch. They had argued that an autonomous Tank Corps was no longer required. Tank Corps advocates at the time failed to present a convincing argument for preserving their semi-independent status.

Pershing and Marshall had articulated their opinion of the '1919 Superior Board' that had been convened to consider the lessons learned from the First World War, and had concluded that 'tanks were accompanying weapons incapable of independent decisive action.' Both Patton and Eisenhower were cautioned in the immediate aftermath of the First World War by their superiors to cease writing about the need for an independent Tank Corps. Eisenhower would later state that he was threatened with court martial proceedings if he persisted in his favourable writings about the Tank Corps.

Infantry Branch Tanks

With the Tank Corps and Tank Board being dissolved in 1920, Patton returned to the cavalry branch the same year and Eisenhower to the infantry branch a couple of years later. Rockenbach remained as commander of the newly-created 'Tank School' at Fort Meade until 1924. He eventually retired as a commander of an artillery unit. The bulk of the light tanks and remaining tankers of the former Tank Corps were distributed in company-size units to US Army and National Guard infantry divisions spread across the country. With the Tank Board disbanded in 1920, the Tank School took over the board's responsibilities for the creation of training and doctrinal manuals.

The Tank School at Fort Meade possessed both a heavy and light tank battalion for training infantry officers in the capabilities and tactics of the vehicles. There were no medium tanks then standardized (approved for production) by the US Army at that time, only experimental tanks classified as mediums. The First World War-vintage heavy tanks were pulled from US Army service in 1932.

The Tank School at Fort Meade was moved to Fort Benning, Georgia, the home of the infantry branch, in 1932. Training activities were hobbled by understrength infantry units and the continued mechanical unreliability of the existing inventory of tanks. Little thought was given to what the future held for the tank.

In 1938, the US Army infantry branch was reorganized. The individual tank companies attached to infantry divisions were done away with and consolidated at Fort Benning to form two tank battalions, overseen by the 68th Infantry Regiment (Light Tanks). It was in turn assigned to a general headquarters pool that would in theory attach a tank battalion to an infantry division when required. How they were to be used on the battlefield continued to reflect their historic role on the battlefields of the First World War as is evident in this passage from an April 1938 War Department directive:

> In the attack, the leading echelon advances closely behind the supporting fire of the artillery and heavy infantry weapons. These tanks, with the support of the other weapons, have the mission of dominating the anti-tank guns. The second echelon, closely followed by the foot troops, advances with the mission of dominating the enemy's machine guns. These are the accompanying tanks that break into the hostile position with the infantry.

To provide these new infantry tank battalions with a more up-to-date doctrine that would incorporate all the latest tactical trends and technology (radios), the Tank School started work on a new manual in 1939 that was still awaiting War Department approval for publication a year later. The 1938 reorganization of the infantry branch and its tanks was proving somewhat problematic by 1940 for a couple of reasons. Firstly, the tank battalions lacked the organic resources (maintenance and repair elements) to operate independently; secondly, they were no longer being trained alongside the infantrymen they were intended to support in battle.

Cavalry Branch Tanks

In spite of the demise of the Tank Corps and the transfer of all its assets and personnel to the infantry branch, various entities within the US Army conducted studies in the 1920s that looked at overseas developments in both tank technology and doctrine. One of them was the British Army Experimental Mechanized Forces, which was in existence from 1927 to 1929. At that time, the word 'mechanization' meant the employment of wheeled or tracked vehicles for combat purposes.

Another word in popular use in the 1920s was 'motorization', which referred to wheeled and tracked vehicles being employed by the military for other than combat use, such as logistical support or moving personnel from place to place.

In 1927, the American Secretary of War Dwight F. Davis had a chance to see the British Army Experimental Mechanized Force during training manoeuvres. He was so impressed by what he saw that he ordered the formation of a temporary American counterpart at Fort Meade in 1928. His vision of tanks performing many more roles than just infantry support was slowly gathering backing among some in the senior levels of the US Army.

One of those who saw a bright future for tanks was Brigadier General Frank Parker (Assistant Chief of Staff for Operations and Training). He submitted a memo in 1928 about the possibility of tanks becoming not just a tactical instrument of warfare but an arm of strategic decision. He also wanted all the First World War-vintage tanks replaced by modern tanks and a more permanent American version of the British Army Experimental Mechanized Force to be established.

What was remarkable about the US Army version of the British Army Experimental Mechanized Force was that it was a combined-arms unit (tank, artillery, cavalry and infantry), supported by its own organic (in-house) maintenance and repair elements. This made it self-sufficient and capable of independent operations on the battlefield. Once its mission was completed the US Army Experimental Mechanized Force was disbanded after six weeks with all the participating units returned to their home stations.

The Next Step

In spite of its brief existence, the US Army version of the British Army Experimental Mechanized Force generated interest among some senior-level US Army officers. In August 1930, the Chief of Staff of the US Army, Major General Charles P. Summerall, authorized the creation of a more permanent organization named the 'Mechanized Force'. It was to be based at Fort Eustis, Virginia and continue where the Experimental Mechanized Force left off.

Unfortunately, funding shortfalls meant that only a handful of experimental tanks could be provided when the Mechanized Force was fully organized in November 1930. This forced it to rely on mechanically unreliable First World War-designed tanks during testing. One officer of the Mechanized Force commented on the lack of modern equipment: 'It must be recognized that with obsolete and make-shift equipment but little of real value can be learned as to the proper tactics and technique in the employment of a modern mechanized force.'

Colonel James K. Parson, a visionary officer of the time, was commander of the Tank School at Fort Meade and assigned the field development of the Mechanized Force. He went one step further, drafting a report that called for the formation of an armoured division and expansion to a six-division force. He did not specify which branch of the US Army should be in charge of the mechanized divisions proposed for fear of strong criticism from the infantry and cavalry branches. Summerall congratulated Parson on his initiative but stated that existing funding issues and other modernization needs for the army made the forming of mechanized divisions impossible at that time.

The appointed commanders of the new Mechanized Force were two progressive cavalry officers: Colonel Daniel Van Voorhis and eventually Major Adna R. Chaffee Jr. Both endeavoured to establish how tanks could perform the roles once performed by US Army mounted cavalry. In 1928, when he realized that horse cavalry had no future on the modern battlefield, Chaffee became one of the biggest proponents of mechanization in the US Army.

Chaffee at one point described what he wanted to see in Mechanized Force officers: 'They must be imbued with the spirit of mobility, rapidity of action and simplicity of control.' He went on to state: 'They must be of a progressive, creative mind and not afraid of radical changes.'

As Brigadier General Frank Parker (Assistant Chief of Staff for Operations and Training) had envisioned, Voorhis and Chaffee both saw the Mechanized Force evolving into something larger that could perform both tactical and strategic operations. Inspiration for this belief might have been provided by the German Army's large multi-division exercises of 1926 in which their cavalry branch, using mock-up tanks, prevailed over all the more conventional infantry opponents.

It has been recorded that following the exercises the German Army Third Cavalry Division reported to its headquarters unit that 'battle without tanks is obsolete.' By 1935, the German Army was undertaking corps-level training exercises aimed at developing and refining their evolving armour doctrine. (Corps are command elements that oversee divisions and provide them with supporting units when required.)

Change is in the Air

On 21 November 1930, Major General Douglas MacArthur took the job of chief of staff of the US Army from Summerall and remained in that post until 1935. His views on the army's future differed from his predecessor. With the limited funding allocated to the US Army during the Great Depression, MacArthur decided that the Mechanized Force was a costly luxury the army could ill afford and therefore dissolved it in October 1931.

MacArthur preferred to take what funding was available to mechanize all the US Army's combat branches, with the emphasis on the infantry and cavalry branches, and maintain the army's personnel strength levels. His opinion regarding the role of tanks deployed in conjunction with infantry appeared in a May 1931 mechanization policy document:

> The infantry mission is to close with the enemy, and its ability and power to accomplish this makes infantry the decisive arm. Its success is a prerequisite to army success; consequently, its efforts must not be dispersed in the performance of auxiliary and supporting missions that can be carried out by other arms. As one of the principal duties of the tank will be to support infantry, it should be trained with it to develop the most efficient type of machines and most applicable methods of tank support for infantry units.

Some of the assets and personnel from the now defunct Mechanized Force were transferred to the unhorsed 1st Cavalry Regiment, which eventually became the 1st Cavalry Regiment (Mechanized). Van Voorhis and Chaffee respectively assumed the roles of commander and executive officer in the newly-mechanized unit. Van

Voorhis left in 1934 for another command and was replaced by Chaffee as commanding officer.

That same year Chaffee transferred back to the War Department General Staff. From that position, he kept up a steady stream of funding for mechanization of the cavalry branch, despite resistance of many reactionary officers within the cavalry branch who saw it as a threat to their beloved horses. Since the National Defense Act of 1920 only allowed the infantry branch to have tanks, the cavalry branch juggled semantics and was able to employ tanks by referring to them as 'combat cars'. Camp Knox, Kentucky became the new home of the 1st Cavalry Regiment (Mechanized). With their presence, the installation became a permanent US Army post, renamed 'Fort Knox' in 1932.

Mechanization Begins

Fort Knox became the centrepiece of the army's mechanization efforts during the period 1933 to 1939. The unhorsed 13th Cavalry Regiment (Mechanized) in 1936 joined the 1st Cavalry Regiment (Mechanized), coming under the command of the 7th Cavalry Brigade (Mechanized) formed in 1932. Joining them in 1935 was the 1st Battalion of the 68th Field Artillery Regiment. These units, along with a number of other supporting units from different branches, made the brigade the only combined-arms unit in the US Army.

The 7th Cavalry Brigade (Mechanized) pioneered new tactics and doctrine for mechanized combined-arms operations, which were applied during multi-division training exercises in the 1930s with great success. Based on positive reviews of their accomplishments during a 1936 training exercise, the then commander of 7th Cavalry Brigade (Mechanized) asked the US Army Chief of Staff, General Marlin Craig, a cavalryman, for authorization to form a mechanized cavalry division but this request was denied. The French Army, by comparison, had established its first mechanized cavalry division in the previous year.

Craig's biggest concern was that division of the development of tanks and doctrine between the infantry and cavalry branches hindered their evolution into something larger and more effective. He therefore directed his staff to study the US Army's mechanization policy in 1937. Their report concluded that MacArthur's 1931 policy decision to mechanize all the combat branches at the same time had been a mistake and recommended that all available resources be devoted to re-establishing an independent mechanized force subordinate to neither the infantry nor cavalry branches. Another recommendation was for the formation of a tank division composed of three mechanized cavalry regiments.

Due to strong opposition from the infantry branch, the staff report's recommendations were not implemented. In 1938 Craig did, however, issue a directive which acknowledged that the new independent, self-sufficient mechanized cavalry forces, such as the 7th Cavalry Brigade (Mechanized), would be able to undertake long-range strategic actions on their own. In effect, he was opening the door to the formation of a mechanized cavalry division, something that Chaffee and Van Voorhis had strongly advocated for some time. In 1939 Voorhis, now a major general, once again pushed to have a mechanized cavalry division formed but with no success. In 1939, on the eve of the Second World War, the Polish Army had a larger mechanized force than its US counterpart.

The naysayers within the US Army who strongly objected to the 7th Cavalry Brigade (Mechanized) and the doctrine it preached had to check themselves when the German Army successfully invaded and conquered Poland in the space of just a few weeks beginning on 1 September 1939. Their victory was largely based on a war of operational manoeuvre (*bewegungskrieg*), similar to the principles of mechanized warfare then being practised by the 7th Cavalry Brigade (Mechanized).

Chaffee addressed the significance of the German invasion of Poland in a late 1939 article in the *Cavalry Journal* to alert his fellow officers to the need for further mechanization of the US Army with the suggestion that up to three mechanized cavalry divisions be formed:

> Prior to September 1939, the question as to what part mechanization was destined to play in large-scale modern warfare was largely an academic one. This question, however, was answered most conclusively on the battlefields of Poland within a few days after the close of the 1st Army Maneuvers, when the German Army, using its mechanized divisions so successfully and decisively conquered a valiant army of a million men in the amazingly short period of two weeks. The lessons brought out by the maneuvers of the 1st Army and other such maneuvers have been confirmed by war.

Despite the events in Poland, some in the senior levels of the US Army leadership dismissed the importance of what had occurred by blaming it on a second-rate Polish Army. Both the leaders of the cavalry and infantry branches of the US Army continued to engage in their long-running inter-service rivalries, preventing Chaffee's formation of three mechanized cavalry divisions from standing a chance. The German Army had formed its first three armoured divisions, popularly known as 'panzer' divisions, in 1935; a measure of how far behind the US Army was lagging. By the time of the 1939 invasion the German Army had six panzer divisions in service and more were planned.

Testing the Concept of Armoured Divisions

In May 1940, the US Army conducted a large-scale multi-division training exercise in Louisiana involving nearly 70,000 men. Referred to as the 'Third Army Manoeuvres', the exercise included the 'Provisional Tank Brigade' organized in January 1940 at

Fort Benning and all the infantry branch's tank units. There was also the 7th Cavalry Brigade (Mechanized) joined with the truck-mounted 6th Infantry Regiment. As Brigadier General Chaffee would comment a month before the training exercise:

> A month ago … as an upshot [to] some missionary work in the War Department I will have the Sixth Infantry in trucks attached to the Brigade for the period of the Third Army Maneuvers … So little by little we are getting the troops, if not the name and dignity of a mechanized division.

The May 1940 training exercise sought to demonstrate/evaluate whether mechanized divisions could be created on an ad hoc basis, depending on battlefield requirements, from smaller units such as battalions, brigades and regiments. By the conclusion of the exercise it was clear to all present that only permanent mechanized divisions in which all the various elements had trained together would be viable on the modern battlefield.

A Breakthrough

Following the May 1940 training exercise, a number of far-sighted US Army officers – including Patton, one of the umpires – talked about what had been learned. The meeting was overseen by Brigadier General Frank Andrews, the US Army War Department chief of operations. Their shared conclusion was that all the existing mechanized cavalry and infantry tank units must be restructured in a new organization referred to as the 'Armoured Force', which would consist of armoured divisions capable of independent operations. The term Armoured Force was intended as a break from the past and because the infantry branch wished to retain the term 'tank' and the cavalry branch the term 'mechanized'.

The successful German invasion of France (led by ten panzer divisions) was a major shock to the senior leadership of the US Army. Beginning the offensive on 19 May 1940, in less than seven weeks the German Army had forced the surrender of the French Army, the latter then considered the finest in the world and the best-equipped.

The quick defeat of the French Army led General Andrews to impress upon the chief of staff of the US Army, George C. Marshall, that the US Army badly needed a new separate armoured force in the same mold as the German Army's panzer force. Marshall concurred, despite strong opposition from the infantry and cavalry branches, and on 10 June 1940 the Armoured Force officially came into existence.

From a March 1942 US Army publication titled *Armored Force, Field Manual, Tactic and Technique* is this passage describing the role of the Armoured Force:

> The role of the Armored Force and its components is the conduct of highly mobile ground warfare, primarily offensive in character, by self-sustaining units

> of great power and mobility, composed of specially equipped troops of the required arms and services. Combat elements of the Armored Force operate in close cooperation with combat aviation and with large units of ground troops in the accomplishment of a mission.

The Armoured Force was not to be officially labelled as a new branch of the US Army (which in reality it was) to prevent the existing infantry and cavalry branches' leadership becoming too incensed. Rather, the Armoured Force was to be referred to as a 'service test' to centralize all mechanized development in the US Army. This was also done as it did not need to be initiated by an act of Congress.

The Armoured Force was renamed the 'Armoured Command' in 1943. In 1944, the Armoured Command became the 'Armoured Centre'. It took until 28 June 1950 before 'Armour' became a separate branch of the US Army.

(**Opposite, above**) The first production British Army heavy tank was labelled the Mark I and had its combat debut on 15 September 1916. Pictured here is an example of a later-production Mark IV model with the classic rhomboidal shape that identified all the British Army heavy tanks of the First World War. As it is fitted with quick-firing (QF) 6-pounder guns, it would be labelled a 'male tank'. *(Tank Museum)*

(**Opposite, below**) Seen here on display is a British-built Mark IV heavy tank. The configuration of the sponson identifies this particular vehicle as having been intended for the fitting of machine guns only. Those Mark IV heavy tanks armed with machine guns were referred to as 'females'. When armed with a QF 6-pounder on one side and a machine gun on the other, the tank would be labelled a 'hermaphrodite' or 'composite'. *(Author's collection)*

102
2324

The most successful tank design of the First World War was the FT Light Tank seen here in Second World War German markings. The two-man tank could be armed with either a single machine gun as seen on this example or with a 37mm main gun. Renault designed the FT Light Tank, building more than half of those manufactured. Other French companies would join in building the FT Light Tank to meet increased demand from the French Army. *(Pierre-Olivier Buan)*

The preserved FT Light Tank seen here weighed approximately 14,000lb. Maximum armour thickness on the cast-armour turreted versions as seen here was 22mm. Armour thickness on the riveted turrets for the FT Light Tank was only 16mm. Maximum speed was just under 5mph and it had a range of about 25 miles. It is 16ft in length, has a width of 5ft 7in and a height of 7ft. *(Pierre-Olivier Buan)*

The imposing figure seen in this picture is General John J. Pershing, commander of the American Expeditionary Forces (AEF) in France. In response to a number of suggestions, he gave approval for the formation of a Tank Corps in December 1917. The first American infantrymen arrived in France in June 1917, with their introduction to combat occurring in October 1917. *(National Archives)*

General John J. Pershing placed Colonel Samuel D. Rockenbach, seen here as a brigadier general, as commander of the newly-formed AEF Tank Corps in December 1917, which at the time had no tanks. Rockenbach had served under Pershing during the Pancho Villa expedition, which took place between 14 March 1916 and 7 February 1917. *(National Archives)*

With no one in the US Army having any experience with tanks, General John J. Pershing chose George S. Patton, seen here posed in front of an FT Light Tank, to attend classes at a French Army tank school with a number of other US Army personnel. Upon completion, he and the others were to establish and operate a new US Army Light Tank School located in Bourg, France. *(Patton Museum)*

Between March and June 1918, the French Army delivered to the US Army Light Tank School an initial batch of twenty-five FT Light Tanks. All were mild-steel, pre-production units, a preserved example of which is seen here. The 150 units of the soft-steel pre-production model were built by Renault and can be identified by having a very small cast-steel armour turret, which was enlarged on production units. *(Tank Museum)*

Shown on display here at a European museum is a restored machine-gun-armed version of the FT Light Tank, fitted with the larger one-man production cast-armour turret. With the AEF Tank Corps, the FT Light Tank first saw combat on 12 September 1918. In total, the US Army would acquire approximately 214 production units of the FT Light Tank during the First World War, not counting the 25 soft-steel training tanks. *(Pierre-Olivier Buan)*

(**Opposite, above**) The extremely colourful camouflage paint scheme on the tank pictured here was applied by the museum staff. It duplicates what would have been typically applied at the factory before the tank was issued to the French Army during the First World War. The combat debut of the FT Light Tank in French Army service occurred on 31 May 1918. *(Pierre-Olivier Buan)*

(**Opposite, below**) On display at a US Army museum is a preserved FT Light Tank that has been painted like the French factory-applied camouflage paint scheme applied during the First World War. It features the tactical markings of the AEF Tank Corps. The two US Army tank battalions equipped with the FT Light Tank had an authorized strength of seventy-five vehicles apiece. *(Oleg Sapunkov)*

(**Above**) An AEF Tank Corps FT Light Tank in France is shown here after encountering an improvised German Army anti-tank mine. On the top of the tank's turret is the vehicle commander's fixed cupola, which also acted as a ventilation dome. The surviving production FT Light Tanks acquired by the AEF Tank Corps from the French Army were eventually shipped back to the United States following the November 1918 armistice. *(Patton Museum)*

Shown here taking part in an historical military vehicle event is a British Army Mark V heavy tank. The semaphore device on the roof of the approximately 65,000lb tank was employed to communicate orders between vehicles as they lacked radios. The British Army would supply the AEF Tank Corps with forty-seven units of the Mark V heavy tank by October 1918. They would go into action for the first time on 29 September 1918. *(Tank Museum)*

At the conclusion of the First World War, the AEF Tank Corps began preparations to ship back all the surviving British Army-supplied Mark V heavy tanks to the United States. The British Army provided an additional ten units. Pictured here at Camp Meade, Maryland, after the First World War is a Mark V model minus any armament. The tank had a top speed of 5mph. *(Patton Museum)*

Shown here at Camp Meade, post-First World War, is a British-built Mark V heavy tank. As no more than thirty-two were brought back to the United States and with no supply of spare parts on hand, the Tank Corps felt it lacked enough of them for any meaningful training purposes. It was decided to place all of them into storage, despite their being considered more reliable than the post-war heavy tank that replaced them. *(Patton Museum)*

Rather than building a modified version of the French FT Light Tank as desired by the AEF Tank Corps, the US Army Ordnance Department decided it wanted something more affordable that could be built by the country's automotive industry. The result was the construction of the Ford 3-ton tank seen here. The AEF Tank Corps was not impressed with the results and only 15 were built before the contract for 15,000 production units was cancelled. *(Author's collection)*

(**Above**) During the First World War the Pioneer Tractor Company was provided with funding by the US Army for the construction of a prototype seen here labelled the 'Skeleton Tank'. It was intended to be a very affordable vehicle, combining the light weight of the French FT Light Tank and the off-road mobility of the British rhomboid-shaped heavy tanks. However, the war came to an end before it could be tested and subsequently, the project was dropped. *(Christophe Vallier)*

(**Opposite, above**) Belonging to the US Army museum system is this Mark VIII heavy tank, which is seen here in storage at Fort Benning, Georgia. The approximately 87,000lb vehicle was intended for use during the First World War by the AEF Tank Corps. However, a completed prototype did not appear until September 1918 and no production units would see service before the fighting ended in France on 11 November 1918 with the Armistice. *(Rob Cogan)*

(**Opposite, below**) The preserved Mark VIII heavy tank seen here was a co-production vehicle designed by the British with the manufacturing of components to take place in both the United States and England, with final assembly at a brand-new factory in France. When the fighting came to an end in November 1918, there were only seven completed examples of the vehicle in England and 100 unassembled kits. *(Paul and Loren Hannah)*

An interior photograph of a preserved Mark VIII heavy tank at a US Army museum. The US Army purchased all of the 100 unassembled kits of the tank in England following the end of the First World War. They were shipped to the United States to be assembled between January and June 1920. As the tanks proved unreliable in use they were seldom employed and were finally placed in storage in 1932. *(Paul and Loren Hannah)*

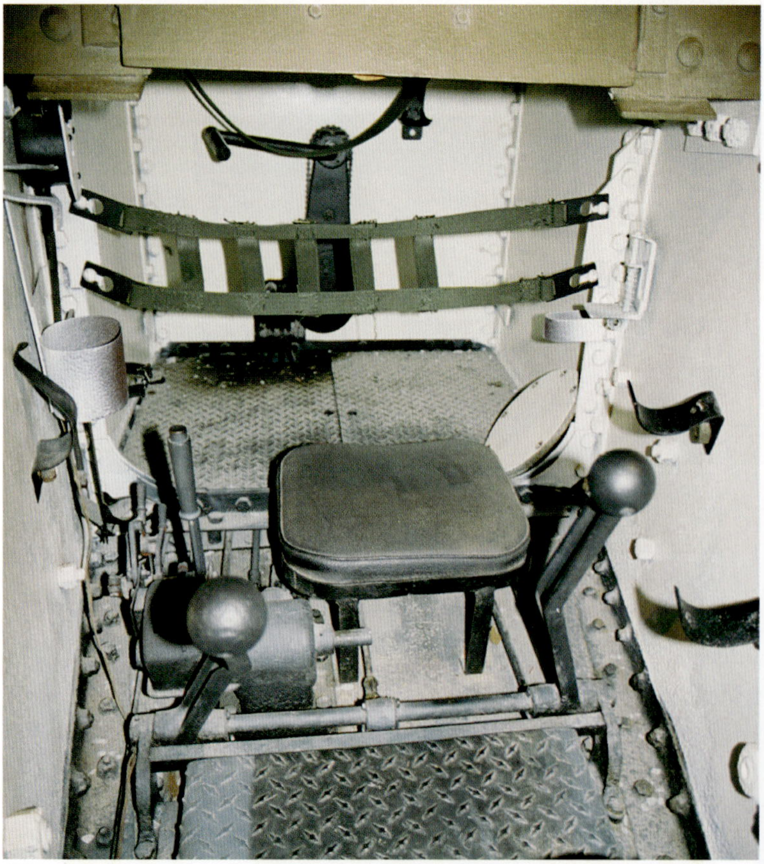

The interior of a preserved 6-ton M1917 Light Tank. At the end of 1917, Renault shipped a single example of its FT Light Tank to the United States as a template from which American industry planned to build 4,400 units of a modified version for the AEF Tank Corps. It was labelled the 6-ton M1917 Light Tank and weighed approximately 14,500lb. *(Rob Cogan)*

Show here is a preserved example of the modified French tank design in storage at Fort Benning, Georgia. There had been high hopes that the first production units of the American-modified version would arrive in France by April 1918. Unfortunately, these plans were not to be realized as the first batch of 6-ton M1917 Light Tanks did not leave the assembly lines until October 1918. None reached France before the Armistice of 11 November 1918. *(Rob Cogan)*

744A

(**Opposite, above**) In total, American factories built 952 units of the 6-ton M1917 Light Tank between 1918 and 1920. Of that number 372 were armed with a 37mm main gun and 526 were armed with machine guns, the rest being unarmed radio-equipped command vehicles. Seen here at Camp Meade, Maryland in 1919 are Major Dwight D. Eisenhower and a posed 6-ton M1917 Light Tank. *(Patton Museum)*

(**Opposite, below**) Unlike the French FT Light Tanks that had rolled off the production line with either a face-hardened riveted armoured turret or a cast-armour turret, the 6-ton M1917 Light Tanks built for the US Army had only face-hardened riveted turrets as seen here on this restored example. Unlike the large steel-rimmed wooden idlers of the FT Light Tank, the 6-ton M1917 Light Tanks had all-steel idlers as is evident in this picture. *(Marc Sehring)*

(**Above**) Like the French FT Light Tank upon which it was based, the 6-ton M1917 Light Tank was mechanically unreliable. Its all-steel tracks had an operational lifespan of less than 100 miles. To prolong their lifespan, they were transported by truck as seen here to their training sites. There were efforts post-war to improve the performance of the 6-ton M1917 Light Tank but all foundered due to lack of funding. *(Patton Museum)*

(**Above**) With funding extremely limited following the First World War, the US Army quickly placed all the FT Light Tanks it had shipped from France to the United States in storage. The US Army's inventory of 6-ton M1917 Light Tanks lasted in service with National Guard units until the late 1930s. Pictured here is a California National Guard 6-ton M1917 in 1933. *(Patton Museum)*

(**Opposite, above**) A serious problem for First World War-era tanks was the short lifespan of their all-steel tracks. American inventor J. Walter Christie saw a way around that by his development of tanks that could be operated with or without tracks. This novel concept caught the attention of the US Army Ordnance Department, which tested the Christie M1919 Medium Tank seen here and a follow-on model labelled the M1921 between 1921 and 1923. They were both rejected as their reliability was poor. *(Patton Museum)*

(**Opposite, below**) In the immediate aftermath of the First World War the Ordnance Department, supported by Rockenbach, believed that medium tanks were more useful than light tanks. This led to the construction of the experimental Medium Tank M1921. It was in turn replaced by the progressively-improved experimental Medium Tank M1922 seen here. Both were powered by a marine engine which proved unsuitable for tanks. *(Patton Museum)*

U.S. ARMY
MED. TANK
MOD. A
1922
U.S. ARMY
21972

ORDNANCE DEPARTMENT, A. P. G.
27487 - 12/30/30.
Medium Tank T-2. Left
front view.

(**Opposite, above**) Pictured here is the experimental Medium Tank T1, constructed in 1927. It was powered by a new dedicated tank engine but still considered underpowered. In spite of this underpowered engine, it was approved for production (referred to as being standardized) on 2 February 1928 as the Medium Tank M1. This standardization was cancelled a short time later due to lack of funding and it once again became the Medium Tank T1. *(Patton Museum)*

(**Opposite, below**) On the heels of the cancelled Medium Tank T1 there appeared the Medium Tank T2 seen here. The three-man vehicle went through trials between December 1930 and January 1932. Due to funding shortfalls, the vehicle was not approved for standardization. Like the Medium Tank T1, the Medium Tank T2 ended its career as a test bed for components and accessories to be fitted to future tank designs. *(Patton Museum)*

(**Above**) The first post-First World War designed-and-built light tank to be tested for consideration by the US Army infantry branch was the T1 pilot in September 1927. It had a front hull-mounted engine and was followed by the improved T1E1, which weighed approximately 16,000lb. It was in turn superseded by the T1E2 seen here. Top speed was about 18mph. None were standardized. *(Ordnance Museum)*

The front hull-mounted engines for the T1 and T1E2 Light Tanks proved unpopular. It was therefore decided to relocate the engine to the rear of the follow-on pilot vehicle, creating the T1E4 Light Tank and later the T1E6 Light Tank seen here. The T1E6 was fitted with a more powerful engine than its predecessors and had a maximum speed of 20mph. Neither vehicle was standardized. *(Patton Museum)*

With the disbanding of the Tank Corps in 1920 and the transfer of all its assets to the infantry branch, there was little thought of tanks being anything other than an infantry support weapon. This narrow view began to broaden in the late 1920s and eventually resulted in the formation of a combined-arms unit named the 'Mechanized Force' in August 1930. Colonel Daniel Van Voorhis, pictured here as a three-star lieutenant general, was appointed as its original commanding officer. *(Patton Museum)*

(**Left**) Appointed second-in-command of the Mechanized Force in July 1931 was Major Adna R. Chaffee, Jr. He is seen here in 1941 as a two-star major general wearing a Rawlings pattern tank helmet, patterned after the company's leather football helmets. Chaffee, like Voorhis and other interwar US Army officers, had seen combat in the First World War and was convinced of the potential of the tank. *(Patton Museum)*

(**Right**) The bringing together of like-minded officers in the Mechanized Force allowed for some thought being given to the development of a suitable doctrine for combined-arms mechanized units. Sadly, as a cost-saving measure, the new chief of staff of the US Army, three-star Lieutenant General Douglas MacArthur, shown here, dissolved the Mechanized Force on 31 October 1931. *(National Archives)*

Upon the disbanding of the Mechanized Force, most of its personnel and assets were transferred the next day to what eventually became the 1st Cavalry (Mechanized). It continued where the Mechanized Force had left off. Pictured here is a J. Walther Christie designed-and-built vehicle he labelled the M1931. Four were acquired by the cavalry branch, which designated them the 'T1 Combat Car' for evaluation. *(Patton Museum)*

The infantry branch tested three examples of the J. Walther Christie M1931 vehicle. They referred to it as the Convertible Medium Tank T3. The word 'convertible' in the vehicle's designation referred to its ability to operate with or without tracks, seen in this picture with tracks installed. Neither the cavalry nor infantry branches elected to procure the M1931, partially due to their high cost relative to Ordnance Department developed-and-built vehicles. *(Patton Museum)*

In spite of the infantry and cavalry branches not wanting the J. Walther Christie Convertible Medium Tank T3, the branches remained interested in the concept of convertible (wheel/track) vehicles. This led to the building of five test vehicles, one of which is seen here, designated the Medium Tank T3E2. It was wider than the Christie T3 and therefore had a four-man crew and thicker armour. Five were built, but the design never went into production as it had serious design flaws. *(Patton Museum)*

Military interest in the concept of convertible (wheel/track) vehicles extended to armoured cars. This led the Ordnance Branch to build the machine-gun-armed T2 Combat Car in 1932. The design of the three-man vehicle was badly flawed so the Ordnance Department came up with the improved T2E1 Combat Car seen here. It also proved unsatisfactory and the concept of a convertible (wheel/track) armoured car was dropped. *(Patton Museum)*

Pictured here is an M1 Armoured Car belonging to the 1st Cavalry Regiment (Mechanized) during a 1934 training exercise. The unit formed part of the 7th Cavalry Brigade (Mechanized) formed in 1932. Twenty units of the three-man armoured car were built between 1931 and 1938. It was armed with a turret-mounted .50 calibre machine gun and a coaxial .30 calibre machine gun. Maximum armour protection on the vehicle was 13mm. *(Patton Museum)*

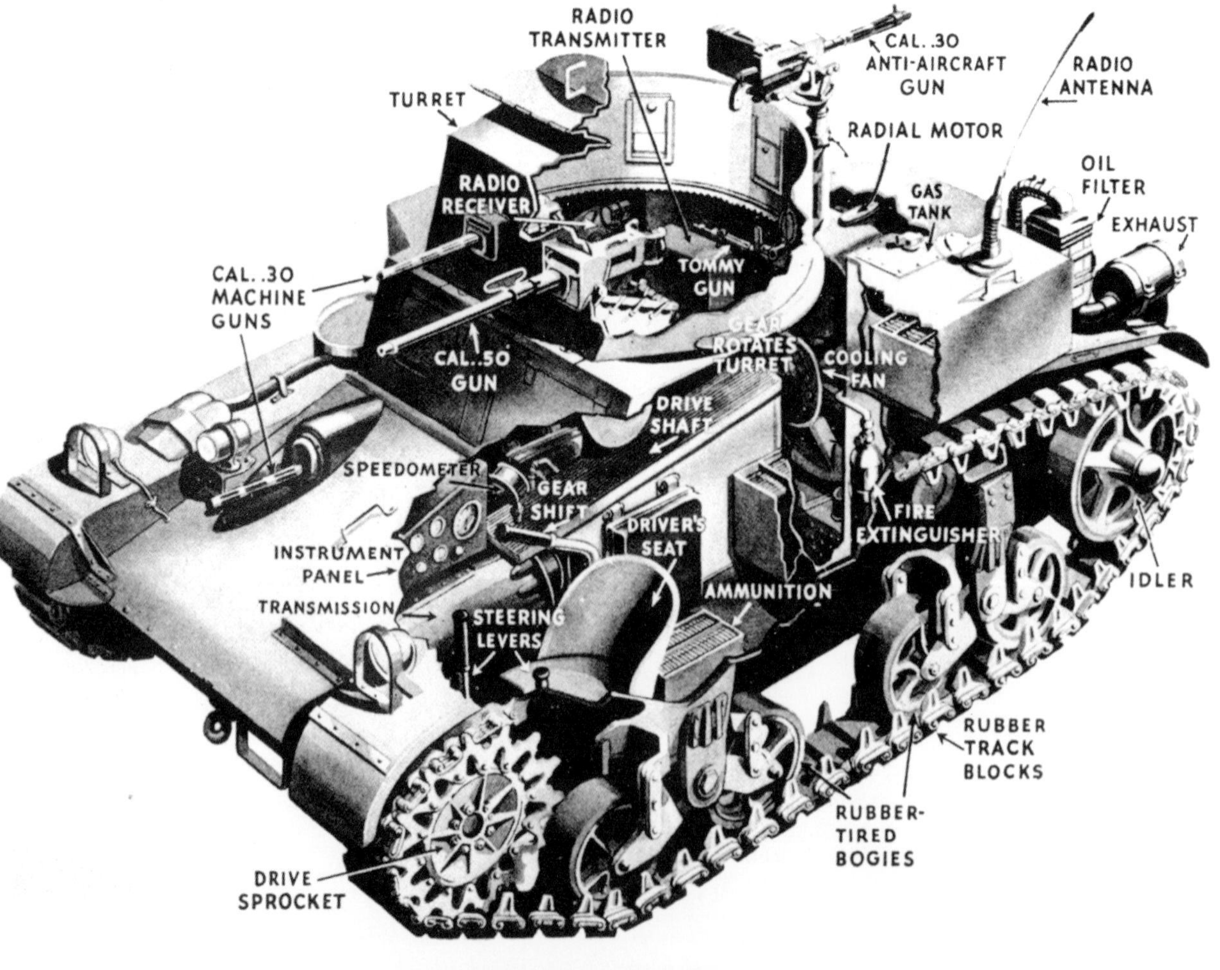
RADIO TRANSMITTER
CAL. .30 ANTI-AIRCRAFT GUN
RADIO ANTENNA
TURRET
RADIAL MOTOR
OIL FILTER
RADIO RECEIVER
GAS TANK
EXHAUST
CAL. .30 MACHINE GUNS
TOMMY GUN
GEAR ROTATES TURRET
CAL. .50 GUN
COOLING FAN
DRIVE SHAFT
SPEEDOMETER
GEAR SHIFT
FIRE EXTINGUISHER
INSTRUMENT PANEL
DRIVER'S SEAT
IDLER
AMMUNITION
TRANSMISSION
STEERING LEVERS
RUBBER TRACK BLOCKS
RUBBER-TIRED BOGIES
DRIVE SPROCKET

(**Opposite, above**) In August 1933 approval was given to construct a pilot light tank, designated the Combat Car T5, pictured here. The four-man vehicle had two turrets, each to be armed with a machine gun, which are not seen fitted to this model. It had a controlled differential steering system and rode on a US Army Ordnance Department-developed vertical volute spring suspension (VVSS) system. The tracks were all-steel. *(Patton Museum)*

(**Above**) Continued development of the Combat Car T5 led to the fielding of the four-man Combat Car M1 seen here. The government-owned Rock Island Arsenal built eighty-nine units of the approximately 19,000lb machine-gun-armed vehicle between 1935 and 1937. It had no vehicle commander's cupola; rather, there was a turret roof consisting of a triple-sectioned hinged cover that could be folded down for protection from overhead threats. *(Patton Museum)*

(**Opposite, below**) Seen here is a cut-away illustration of the Combat Car M1. Unlike the all-steel tracks of the Combat Car T5, the production M1 Combat Car rode on the new double-pinned, rubber-blocked tracks. It weighed approximately 19,000lb and had a maximum speed on level paved roads of 45mph. Off-road it could maintain speeds of between 15 and 20mph. *(Patton Museum)*

U.S.A. W-30261

(**Opposite, above**) In spite of the design failures of both the cavalry branch's T1 and T2/T2E1 Combat Cars, work continued on the concept of convertible (wheel/track) vehicles. This would result in the construction of the T4 Convertible Combat Car in 1933. Changes to the design resulted in the building of the four-man T4E1 Combat Car seen here. The cavalry branch wanted the T4E1 placed into production but that idea was rejected in favour of the more affordable T5 Combat Car. *(Patton Museum)*

(**Above**) The chief of the infantry branch had seen the T4 Combat Car undergoing testing and was impressed. He therefore proposed a better armoured version for the infantry branch, which became the Convertible Medium Tank T4, sixteen of these being built. A preserved example is seen here in storage at Fort Benning, Georgia. It had a top speed on its wheels of approximately 38mph. *(Rob Cogan)*

(**Opposite, below**) In addition to the turreted T4 Combat Car, there were three examples built of a non-turreted version seen here designated the Medium Tank T4E1. Both it and the Medium Tank T4 were recommended for standardization in 1936 but this was rejected due to production costs. In March 1939 both the T4 and T4E1 were once again recommended for standardization. This was approved and they became the Medium Tank M1. *(Patton Museum)*

U.S.A.
W 40223

ROCK ISLAND ARSENAL
731-40034 Nov. 13, 1934
Tank, Light, T2.

(**Opposite, above**) The Cavalry Board had rejected the T1 Combat Car. However, they remained interested in the vehicle's ability to operate at high speeds without its tracks. This eventually led to the construction in 1938 of the Convertible Combat Car T7 shown here. It consisted of an M1 Combat Car fitted with six oversized road wheels, three on either side of the hull. Test results were not positive and it was cancelled on 19 October 1939. *(Patton Museum)*

(**Opposite, below**) At the same time that the cavalry branch was working on the T5 Combat Car, the infantry branch was working on the very similar single-turreted T2 Light Tank seen here. Originally fitted with a British-inspired suspension system, testing showed it to be inferior to the US Army Ordnance Department-developed vertical volute spring suspension (VVSS) system seen here fitted to the vehicle. Improvements to the T2 Light Tank resulted in the designation T2E1. *(Patton Museum)*

(**Above**) Improvements to the Combat Car M1 resulted in the construction of the four-man machine-gun-armed Combat Car M2 seen here, which weighed approximately 25,500lb. Thirty-four were built by the Rock Island Arsenal in 1940. It differed from its predecessor due to the trailing idler being lowered. This increased the ground contact length of the ride on the new double-pinned, rubber-blocked tracks and in turn reduced ground pressure. *(Patton Museum)*

(**Above**) After more developmental work on the T2E1 Light Tank seen here, including the fitting of the now standard double-pinned, rubber-blocked tracks to the vehicle, the single-turreted machine-gun-armed vehicle was approved for production and standardized as the M2A1 Light Tank with nine built in 1935. The vehicle had a weight of approximately 19,000lb and a top speed of 45mph. *(Patton Museum)*

(**Opposite, above**) At the same time, the single-turret, machine-gun-armed M2A1 Light Tank was being standardized. The infantry branch decided to standardize a twin-turreted, machine-gun-armed version of the same vehicle labelled originally as the T2E2 Light Tank as seen here as the M2A2 Light Tank. A total of 237 units of the approximately 19,000lb vehicle were built in 1937 at the Rock Island Arsenal. *(Patton Museum)*

(**Opposite, below**) Shown here when it was on display at the now closed Patton Museum of Cavalry and Armor is this weaponless Light Tank M2A3. It is the only surviving example of seventy-three units built in 1938. It had a slightly thicker armour than its predecessors and therefore weighed approximately 21,000lb. There was also a bit more spacing between the two machine-gun-armed turrets compared to the M2A2 Light Tank. *(Rob Cogan)*

C
USA

U.S.A. W-30442

(**Opposite, above**) In December 1938, a single Light Tank M2A3 was taken off the production line and both up-armoured and up-gunned. The resulting vehicle was designated the Light Tank M2A4 and placed into production in May 1940. When production ended in March 1941, a total of 375 units had come across the assembly lines. The approximately 26,000lb M2A4 served only as a training vehicle with the US Army, although thirty-six units did serve with the United States Marine Corps, many of those seeing combat on the island of Guadalcanal. *(Patton Museum)*

(**Above**) The M2A4 Light Tank was armed with the 37mm main gun M3, which had a long under-barrel recoil mechanism. To protect this recoil mechanism an armoured sleeve, which projected outward from the tank's gun shield, was added as seen on the M2A4 pictured here. Subsequent light tanks would be armed with the 37mm main gun M6, which lacked the extended under-barrel recoil mechanism of the 37mm gun M3. *(Patton Museum)*

(**Opposite, below**) Shown here in storage at Fort Benning, Georgia is this early-model M3 Light Tank, with a riveted hull and a partly-welded turret. The M3 Light Tank was a progressively-improved M2A2 Light Tank with thicker frontal armour. A total of 4,526 units of the M3 Light Tank would be built between March 1941 and October 1942. Due to its thicker armour, the M3 Light Tank weighed approximately 28,000lb. *(Rob Cogan)*

(**Above**) Continued improvements to the M3 Light Tank resulted in the production of the M3A1 Light Tank seen here. The newest version of the M3 Light Tank series lacked the vehicle commander's cupola seen on the original version. The M3A1 first rolled off the factory floor in May 1942 and remained in production until February 1943, with a total of 4,621 units completed. *(Pierre-Olivier Buan)*

(**Opposite, above**) A preserved M3A1 Light Tank belonging to the collection of a European museum. The thickest armour on the tank was its cast-armour gun shield at 50mm. The vertical front upper hull came in at 38mm, with the sloping middle hull plate being 16mm thick and the lower front cast-armour hull 44mm thick. The hull sides from top to bottom were 25mm thick. *(Pierre-Olivier Buan)*

(**Opposite, below**) After experimenting in the early 1930s with a number of modified civilian cars for possible employment by the cavalry branch as reconnaissance vehicles, the US Army standardized the Scout Car M1 seen here in 1934. A total of seventy-six units of the approximately 7,600lb vehicle were built between 1934 and 1937. Maximum armour thickness was 13mm. *(Patton Museum)*

TANK
JE BUNKER
IN GROBNICA
Doživetja tankistov
FRANC ŠKRLJ
Po bitki
pri El Alameinu
TOMŠIČ
Med Rimljani

USA W-60243

(**Above**) In 1938, the US Army standardized the Scout Car M2. A total of twenty-two units of the vehicle were built between 1935 and 1938. Following the M2 Scout Car off the production line was the progressively-improved M2A1 Scout Car seen here. Its designation was later changed to Scout Car M3. Some 100 units of the approximately 8,000lb Scout Car M3 were built between 1936 and 1939. *(Patton Museum)*

(**Opposite, above**) In 1939, a redesigned version of the M3 Scout Car appeared as the M3A1, a restored example of which is pictured here. The vehicle weighed approximately 12,000lb and had a maximum armour thickness of 6mm. A total of 20,894 units of the M3A1 Scout Car were built between 1939 and March 1944, with a great many being supplied under Lend-Lease to other armies. *(Pierre-Olivier Buan)*

(**Opposite, below**) In 1936, the Ordnance Department pushed ahead with the development of the five-man Medium Tank T5. Rather than design a new tank from scratch, it was decided to save time by simply enlarging the successful chassis of the Light Tank M2 series. The initial mock-up seen here in 1937 had a wooden upper hull and turret armed with a dummy 37mm main gun. It was labelled the T5 Medium Tank (Phase 1). *(Patton Museum)*

F187028

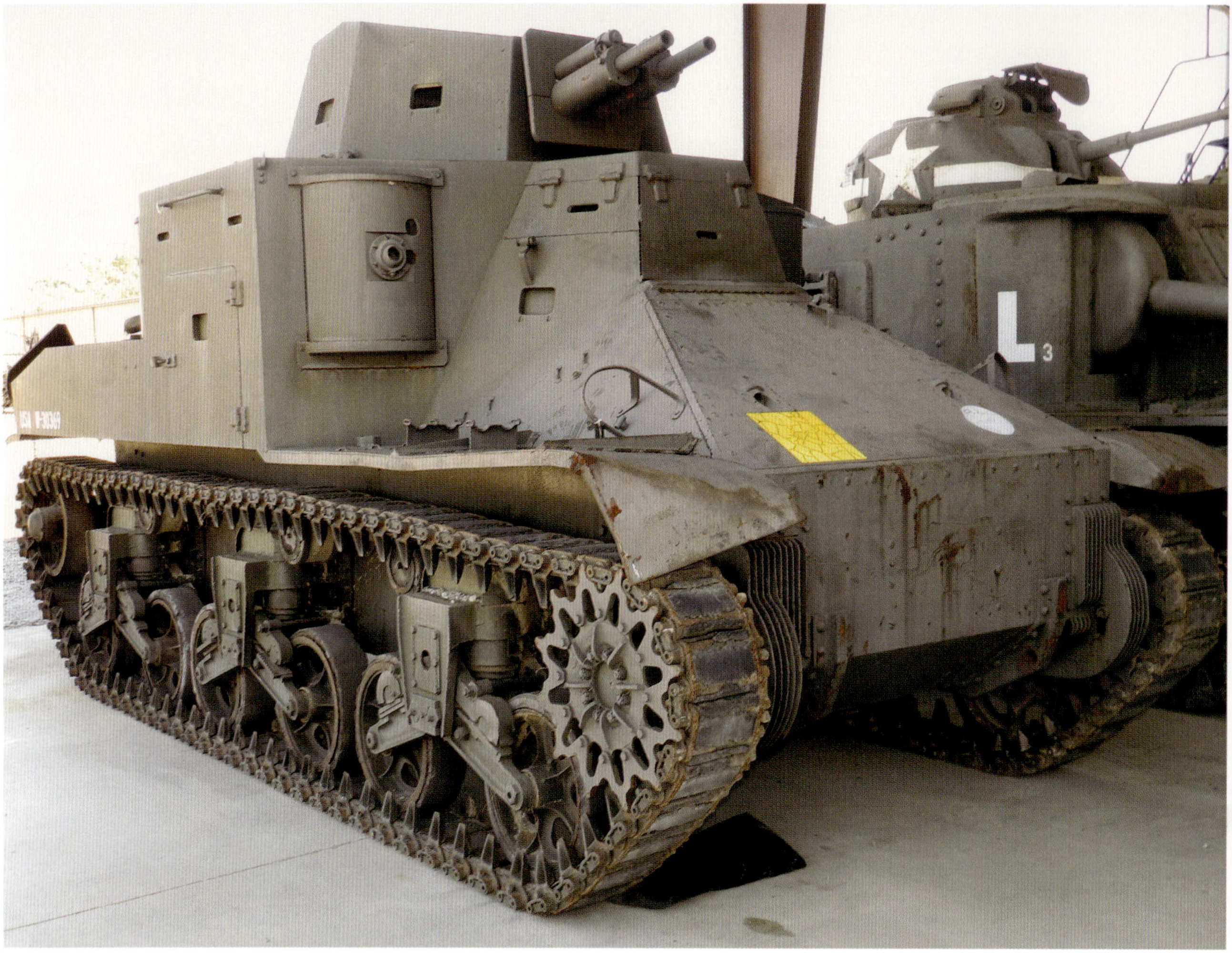

(**Above**) The infantry branch liked what they saw with the mock-up T5 Medium Tank (Phase 1). This led to the construction of the single soft-steel prototype seen here. It was armed with a twin 37mm main gun mount as the new high-velocity single-barrel 37mm gun was not yet ready. Testing of the mild-steel prototype T5 Medium Tank (Phase 1) began in February 1938 and continued until June 1938. *(Rob Cogan)*

(**Opposite, above**) The testing of the mild-steel prototype T5 Medium Tank (Phase 1) went so well that it was standardized as the Medium Tank M2 in June 1938. The approximately 38,000lb tank seen here was now fitted with a single-barrel high-velocity 37mm main gun and up to eight .30 calibre machine guns. Due to continued funding shortfalls, only eighteen units of the Medium Tank M2 were built beginning in 1939. *(Patton Museum)*

(**Opposite, below**) The Medium Tank M2 was armed with the same 37mm gun M3 as fitted to the Light Tank M2A4. Besides the turret-mounted 37mm main gun, the vehicle carried eight .30 calibre air-cooled machine guns. All were in the tank's upper hull. Six were intended for use against ground targets and the remaining two as anti-aircraft guns. *(Patton Museum)*

M-2 MEDIUM TANK -- 1939

By tweaking the design of the Medium Tank M2, the Ordnance Department came up with the improved Medium Tank M2A1 seen here. With the Second World War raging in Europe the US Army was in desperate need of medium tanks and 1,000 units of the M2A1 Medium Tank were ordered in August 1940 from American industry. However, only ninety-four were built by August 1941, when it was cancelled in favour of a new medium tank. *(Rob Cogan)*

Chapter Two

Armoured Divisions Appear

With the formation of the Armoured Force on 10 July 1940, a few weeks after the fall of France, Chaffee (now a brigadier general) was appointed as its first commander. He was also placed in charge of the 1st Armoured Corps. The latter organization copied the German Army's command structure counterpart referred to as the *Panzerkorps* (Tank Corps), which managed several panzer divisions. The Armoured Force leadership was also interested in eventually creating tank armies.

The 1st Armoured Corps was composed of two units created on 15 July 1940: the 1st and 2nd Armoured Divisions. The 1st Armoured Division became known as 'Old Ironsides' and the 2nd as 'Hell on Wheels'. The former was based on an enlarged and reorganized 7th Cavalry Brigade (Mechanized). The latter was created out of the Provisional Tank Brigade located at Fort Benning. The 2nd was reorganized with the same TO&E (Table of Organization and Equipment) as the 1st Armoured Division.

With the exception of two cavalry regiments, all regular US Army mechanized units became part of the Armoured Force. The eighteen individual National Guard tank companies formed in 1920 by the National Defense Act were reorganized into four tank battalions and federalized on 7 September 1940. All former branch designations of the various infantry and cavalry mechanized units were eliminated and the units were redesignated as armoured units. The term 'combat car' disappeared and all the former cavalry branch vehicles were relabelled as light tanks. None would see combat in the Second World War.

Armoured Division Comparisons

The US Army's first two armoured divisions were generally modelled after the pre-war tank-heavy German panzer division TO&E as that was the only information then available. The US Army lacked information on the changes implemented in the panzer divisions' TO&E shortly before the invasion of Poland and subsequent changes based on combat experience from the invasions of Poland and France. The most important was the reduction of the number of tanks and addition of more infantry and other supporting arms to make the divisions a more balanced combined-arms organization that would be capable of undertaking a far wider range of roles.

The TO&E of the two new US Army armoured divisions called for 390 tanks apiece. Their German Army counterparts averaged 324 tanks at the time. The US armoured divisions' tank-heavy arrangement was echoed in the 1940 British Army armoured divisions with 342 tanks. Red Army armoured divisions' TO&Es authorized 350 tanks. By contrast, the pre-German invasion French Army armoured divisions had only 158 tanks each. However, their cavalry branch light mechanized divisions (*Divisions Légère Mécanique or DLMs*) had a strength of 220 tanks apiece.

Armoured Division Problems

Both the 1st and 2nd Armoured Divisions were initially badly hampered by shortages of both tanks and personnel. American industry required considerable time to fully convert from producing civilian goods to producing military weapons and equipment. The construction of tanks, let alone the allocation of scarce materials, also had to compete with higher-priority items such as aircraft, artillery and naval vessels. Compounding the priority problem was the allocation of most of early production to Lend-Lease to the British Army in North Africa, in the light of supply shortfalls, losses and qualitative inferiority of British tanks versus German tanks.

Further difficulty was imposed as the 1st and 2nd Armoured Divisions had to provide training cadres to the new 3rd and 4th Armoured Divisions, which were established on 15 April 1941. The 3rd was officially nicknamed 'Spearhead' and the 4th never took an official nickname. Cadres for the formation of future armoured divisions would be drawn from the future 8th and 20th Armoured Divisions.

The Importance of Fort Knox

The Armoured Force Replacement Training Centre founded at Fort Knox in October 1940 was given responsibility for the training of the armoured division personnel intended for serving in tanks or armoured reconnaissance units. It was renamed the Armoured Replacement Training Centre in 1943.

Instruction for officers assigned to armoured divisions was performed at the 'Armoured School', which began its first training cycle in October 1940 and its last in November 1944. Like the Armoured Force Replacement Training Centre, the Armoured School, which was later renamed Armour School, was located at Fort Knox.

An article in the November/December issue of *Armor Magazine* titled 'Fort Knox: Birthplace of Today's Armor Branch' by Dr Robert S. Cameron explains the importance of Fort Knox to US Army armoured divisions of the Second World War:

> A strong link emerged between the new armored divisions and Fort Knox. All armored doctrine, training guidance, personnel appointments, matériel requirements, and tables of organization and equipment emanated from the

post. New soldiers and replacements also trained at Fort Knox before joining their units. Through its central influence, the Armored Force sought to ensure uniformity in training, doctrine, and adherence to common standards. The direct influence of Fort Knox on armored organizations diminished during World War II, especially after their deployment overseas. However, the Armored Force School remained a nexus for the dissemination of doctrinal updates and combat lessons pertinent to mounted operations.

Participants in the Armoured Replacement Training Centre originally went through a twelve-week training cycle, later extended to seventeen weeks despite the urgent need for trained personnel, before assignment to an armoured division. The brightest were either retained as instructors at Fort Knox or sent off to OCS (Officer Candidate School).

Due to manpower shortages in the European Theatre of Operations (ETO), the seventeen weeks of training was reduced in January 1945 to only fifteen weeks, despite awareness among the senior leadership of the US Army that even seventeen weeks of training did not fully prepare soldiers for their overseas combat assignments.

Armoured Corps Issues

In October 1940 Chaffee pushed for the formation of a 'II Armoured Corps' to oversee the planned raising of the 3rd and 4th Armoured Divisions. However, this request was stymied by the War Department as it considered armoured corps to be unnecessary. Marshall concurred with the War Department view and ordered a halt to the formation of any additional armoured corps.

Chaffee eventually talked Marshall into considering the possibility of more armoured corps. With the creation of additional armoured divisions in 1942 there would eventually be four armoured corps authorized. Yet the I and II Armoured Corps never evolved into true combat formations as they were restricted to training assignments. The III and IV Armoured Corps never had permanent units assigned.

In September 1942, the War Department (the forerunner of today's Department of Defense) decided that instead of specialized corps there would only be generic corps, which could each be configured to command from two to six divisions of any type. The dissolution of armoured corps was made official in August 1943: the 1st Armoured Corps was deactivated in July 1943 and the other three were converted into generic corps headquarters units. By the end of the Second World War the US Army had formed twenty-four generic corps, and a single specialized corps, the XVIII Airborne Corps, formed in August 1944.

The role of the corps commander and staff was to give directions to divisions. One American general described the corps commander as 'the last man towards the rear who directs tactical fire on the enemy. He is the commander who conducts the battle.' The demise of the armoured corps concept also made moot the possibility of US Army armoured armies. The ten US Army armies formed during the Second World War were generic organizations, like the corps assigned to them. Armies were in turn overseen by army groups, three of which were formed during the war years.

Let the Training Begin

In spring 1941, the US Army began laying plans for army versus army war games, which would include the 1st and 2nd Armoured Divisions of the 1st Armoured Corps. The war games would test the readiness of an army as a whole and the leadership skills of its possible future battlefield commanders. The man overseeing the army versus army war games was Brigadier General Lesley McNair (eventually promoted to lieutenant general).

McNair was the chief of staff of the General Headquarters (GHQ) US Army, formed shortly after the Armoured Force. Thus McNair was responsible for development of army doctrine and training in the United States, as well as equipment development and unit organization. In March 1942, the GHQ was renamed 'Headquarters, Army Ground Forces' (AGF). McNair had started his career in the US Army in the cavalry branch but quickly transferred to the ordnance branch.

The divisional war games of May 1941 were quickly followed by corps-level games. The first army versus army war games were labelled the 'Louisiana Manoeuvres' and consisted of two phases, with the first beginning in August 1941 and the second in September. These massive war games took place in an area encompassing approximately 30,000 square miles across the states of Louisiana, Texas and Mississippi.

War Game Issues

The two-phase 1941 Louisiana Manoeuvres were flawed in execution by a number of factors. The biggest problem was McNair's growing belief that anti-tank weapons were the most effective tank-killers, therefore he skewed the rules to confirm this belief.

McNair's belief in the value of anti-tank weapons had first appeared in his writings in the 1930s. In a July 1940 memo, he wrote that in his opinion, it was 'poor economy to use a $35,000.00 medium tank to destroy another tank when the job can be done by a gun [anti-tank] costing a fraction as much.'

McNair's opinion on the relative value of tanks and anti-tank guns had been reinforced by his interpretation of what the French Army had done right and wrong in attempting to stop the German Army panzer divisions in May 1940. What had attracted McNair's attention was the French Army mounting normally towed anti-tank guns on the rear of trucks. The leadership of the Armoured Force espoused the theory that the best tank-killer would be another tank, but to no avail.

Reasons for the Poor Showing

Compounding the problem for the Armoured Force during the 1941 Louisiana Manoeuvres was their generally poor showing. Some of the failures were attributed to its doctrinal deficiencies. Many observers on site mentioned the lack of coordination between the various components of the armoured divisions, each acting independently. This resulted in tank units attacking positions without infantry support, without artillery support, etc. and therefore suffering heavy losses to anti-tank guns.

Another point commented on by the observers and umpires was the fact that the two armoured divisions lacked sufficient infantry to perform many tasks. Supporting infantry could have dealt with the anti-tank guns that took such a toll on the tanks during the war games.

Patton, who had been made commander of the 2nd Armoured Division on 11 April 1941, described the problems to the officers of his division: 'We still fail to use every weapon every time ... Each time we fight with only one weapon when we could use several weapons, we are not winning a battle, we are making fools of ourselves.'

General Marshall forced into retirement a number of high-level officers for what he considered their demonstrated substandard performance. However, Patton and Eisenhower (the latter having recently been promoted to brigadier general shortly before the war games) not only came out with their reputations intact but having made a very favourable impression on all concerned by their different contributions. This would lead them both to much higher command during the Second World War.

New Armoured Force Leadership

Lieutenant General Jacob L. Devers of the artillery branch who had replaced Chaffee (who died of cancer on 22 August 1941) as head of the Armoured Force on 21 August 1941 had his own thoughts on the poor showing of the 1st and 2nd Armoured Divisions. He attributed it to poorly-trained officers and substandard staff work. Devers also recognized, as did others, that the existing 1940 armoured division TO&E was another major reason for the failure of the armoured divisions to coordinate their actions.

The poorly-thought-out 1940 TO&E had been studied before the war games. This would eventually result in plans for a new armoured division TO&E that would emphasize the employment of combined-arms units as normal practice. Insufficient time meant that it could not be implemented before the follow-on 'Carolina Manoeuvres' scheduled to take place between 6 October and 30 November 1941.

Major General Charles Scott, who had been appointed to replace Chaffee as commander of the 1st Armoured Corps, sent out a memo to the divisional commanders of the 1st and 2nd Armoured Divisions just as the Carolina Manoeuvres began. The memo detailed all the tactical mistakes that were made during the previous Louisiana Manoeuvres and how they could be avoided during the present manoeuvres. For example, instead of sending tank columns recklessly down roads to encounter anti-tank guns and be wiped out, the division's tanks were to be kept concealed until infantry and reconnaissance screens had cleared the tanks' intended path of advance.

The 1st and 2nd Armoured Divisions' poor showing in the 1941 Louisiana Manoeuvres soured McNair's opinion on the future value to the US Army of the Armoured Force. From that point on he chose to emphasize the traditional US Army ground combat team of the infantry and artillery branches within the AGF, with the Armoured Force being dramatically reduced in importance. Patton would state upon the conclusion of the war in the ETO that 'I do not have to tell you who won the war. You know the artillery did.'

New Armoured Divisions

In May 1942, it was decided to scale back the number of proposed armoured divisions from sixty-one to forty-seven. The decrease in the number of armoured divisions cannot be blamed completely on McNair. President Franklin D. Roosevelt's staff assessed the production capabilities of American industry – taking into account the massive needs of Britain and the Soviet Union for Lend-Lease equipment, including tanks – and concluded that the proposed number of armoured divisions was unrealistic. This led in 1942 to reducing the number of planned armoured divisions as above and ultimately to only twenty. By the summer of 1943, the number of armoured divisions was further reduced to sixteen. There would eventually be sixty-seven infantry divisions mobilized by the US Army during the Second World War.

In October 1941, the 5th Armoured Division named 'Victory' was formed. The following year nine armoured divisions were created: the 6th 'Super Sixth', the 7th 'Lucky Seven', the 8th 'Thundering Herd', the 9th 'Phantom', the 10th 'Tiger', the 11th 'Thunderbolt', the 12th 'Hellcats', the 13th 'The Black Cats' and the 14th 'Liberator' divisions. Two final armoured divisions were formed in 1943 – the 16th and the 20th – but neither received an official nickname.

The problems that bedevilled the 1st and 2nd Armoured Divisions – shortage of men and equipment – were mirrored in the experience of the follow-on armoured divisions during the rush to field them. The men assigned to an armoured division sometimes had very limited or even no training. The shortage of qualified officers was a serious issue, not just among the new armoured divisions but extending all the way up to the Armoured Force headquarters and Armoured School at Fort Knox.

McNair's Tank Destroyer Detour

McNair's pet project, a proposed semi-independent tank destroyer force, gathered a great deal of attention from their 1941 war-game performance. As McNair had a very close connection to his mentor, chief of staff of the army George C. Marshall, McNair convinced Marshall of a requirement for such a force. This would result in the creation of fifty-one GHQ-level tank destroyer battalions on paper on 3 December 1941. These would later become known as the 'Tank Destroyer Force' and included both towed and self-propelled units.

The envisioned concept was that the Tank Destroyer Force would deal with the massed German tank attacks, which in the US Army's view had led to the fall of France. This would allow US Army armoured division tanks to concentrate on soft (unarmoured) targets such as command posts and artillery positions located behind the enemy's front lines encountered during offensive (exploitation) operations.

Proposals studied in December 1941 envisioned a requirement for 220 tank destroyer battalions. As with the large number of armoured divisions originally proposed, the number of tank destroyer battalions under consideration quickly dropped as a degree of realism crept into what was truly needed and what could be supported logistically overseas.

By early 1943, it was thought that only 143 tank destroyer battalions were required. By the end of the year the number had dropped to 106. Of the 106 tank destroyer battalions eventually formed, 71 went overseas with the other 35 remaining in the United States converted to other roles between December 1943 and May 1944.

The self-propelled anti-tank gun battalions raised for the Tank Destroyer Force were intended to be employed offensively. Their assigned motto became 'Seek, Strike and Destroy'. However, their 1943 combat performance in French North Africa was mixed, with some successes and some failures. In a US Army report by Major General E.N. Harmon (commander of the 1st Armoured Division from April 1943 to July 1944) compiled after the fighting in North Africa and titled 'Notes on Combat Experience during the Tunisian and African Campaign' appears this passage:

> There is no need for tank destroyers. I believe the whole organization and development of the tank destroyer will be considered a great mistake of the war. In the first place, the doctrine originally promulgated, of the tank destroyer seeking out and pursing the tank was a fallacy which caused the destruction of many lives and much equipment before it was corrected.

In spite of the doctrinal failure of the Tank Destroyer Force, the self-propelled tank destroyer battalions of various TO&Es were not wasted by theatre commanders during the Second World War. Rather, many found themselves semi-permanently attached to both infantry and armoured divisions from the North African campaign through the fighting in the ETO. In the immediate aftermath of the Second World War the US Army quickly did away with the Tank Destroyer Force as it now had a well-armoured tank with firepower equal to the best-armed tank destroyer.

Armoured Division Changes

The 1940 armoured division TO&E was fairly simple, with an armoured brigade of 390 tanks divided between three tank regiments of 130 tanks each. Two of the tank regiments were armed with light tanks and the third with medium tanks. Despite the German Army and the Red Army having already decided that medium tanks were the future of armoured warfare, the US Army armoured divisions of 1940 saw its two light tank regiments as the most potent battlefield weapon in its inventory. This belief is seen in a passage from a draft US Army armoured field manual dated July 1941:

> ... due to its organization and equipment [the light tank regiment] is the most mobile, self-contained combat element of the armored division ... Its main role, as part of the armored brigade, is to furnish the striking power necessary for the conduct of highly mobile ground warfare against strategical or tactical objectives deep in the hostile rear.

The single medium-tank regiment of the 1940 armoured division was intended only to reinforce the division's two light tank regiments when encountering enemy tanks or anti-tank guns with both direct and indirect fire. The medium tank regiment was incapable of independent action, since it lacked the reconnaissance and support elements provided to the light tank regiments. The emphasis on light tanks for the 1940 armoured division TO&E also had something to do with the fact that full-scale production of a suitable medium tank did not begin until the autumn of 1941.

Of secondary importance in the scheme of things for the 1940 armoured division was its single armoured infantry regiment (riding on trucks) and a single artillery regiment equipped with towed artillery pieces. While trucks were a mobility improvement over marching infantry and horse-drawn artillery, trucks simply couldn't go where tanks could and towed artillery could not deploy or relocate as quickly as self-propelled artillery. The first armoured half-tracks for transporting armoured infantry did not start coming off the production lines until May 1941. The first armoured self-propelled artillery piece did not begin to come off the assembly line until January 1942.

The infantry and engineer elements of the 1940 armoured division were found in the support echelon, which existed primarily to protect the division's communications lines, secure captured objectives and prepare the way for the strike echelon's decisive attacks. In addition, the 1940 armoured division came with a battalion of engineers and an armoured reconnaissance battalion.

The 1940 armoured division was similar to that of the pre-war German Army panzer divisions, which had 324 tanks. The most important difference was that the tank, infantry and artillery regiments of the US Army armoured division tended to operate as separate entries, as was shown during the Louisiana Manoeuvres. By comparison, in the panzer divisions, the preferred method was to 'task force' the various battalions of a division's regiments into ad hoc *Kampfgruppen* (combat groups) to perform specific missions.

In the US Army Centre of Military History historical monograph titled *The US Army GHQ Maneuvers of 1941* by Christopher R. Gabel is this passage in which the author enumerates the differences that existed between German Army panzer division doctrine and that of the US Army armoured divisions of the same year:

> There is no indication that Chaffee expected infantry, artillery, and armor to fight side by side in the *Kampfgruppe* manner. Overall, the 1940 armored division reveals that Chaffee valued the speed and mobility of his light armored regiments over the firepower, staying power, and protective armor of the other elements, an attitude that was consistent with his cavalry background. Stated simply, the principle of combined arms was not effectively observed.

By the time of the German invasion of the Soviet Union in June 1941, the German Army panzer divisions averaged about 190 tanks. By this time the US Army was aware that no two panzer divisions seemed to have the same TO&E. As Germany lacked the manufacturing capacity to fulfill all requirements, the Wehrmacht had had to issue varying quantities of increasingly inferior Czechoslovak and French designs to its panzer units.

In a June 1941 memo, Brigadier General Alvan C. Gillem Jr, then commander of the 3rd Armoured Division, stressed to Chaffee that 'Our armored divisions should be organized and equipped to be at least the equal of, but preferably superior to, the German armored division.' His opinion, as well as that of many others, led to a near-constant refinement of the 1940 TO&E into a closer imitation of the very successful German panzer divisions. This would eventually lead to a new March 1942 TO&E for armoured divisions.

The 1942 Armoured Division

The 1942 armoured division TO&E called for 380 tanks, divided between two armoured regiments of 190 tanks each. These contained 232 medium tanks and 158 light tanks. Each 1942 armoured division tank regiment was subdivided into three battalions of approximately sixty tanks each, with two battalions of medium and one battalion of light tanks.

The 1942 armoured division TO&E also included a single armoured infantry regiment and a self-propelled armoured artillery regiment. Both were further subdivided into three battalions each. To improve coordination between the three self-propelled armoured artillery battalions, Devers saw to it that a divisional artillery headquarters was added to the 1942 armoured division TO&E. To improve the logistical system of the division, a supply battalion was also added.

Authorized for the 1942 armoured division TO&E were 126 units of a truck-mounted anti-tank gun vehicle. It was the Tank Destroyer Force's first anti-tank platform. These were found in the armoured tank battalions, armoured infantry battalions, armoured field artillery battalions and armoured engineer battalions, as well as the division train.

From an Armoured Force manual is this extract of what was found in the division train: '... maintenance vehicles, and ammunition vehicles, and in some cases company kitchens accompany the battalion. Company maintenance vehicles follow at the tail of each company column. Some fuel and lubricants trucks follow the company column. Ammunition vehicles are grouped at the rear of the battalion.'

Carried over from the 1940 armoured division TO&E was an armoured reconnaissance battalion. One of its main roles is mentioned in this passage from an Armoured Force manual: 'The division reconnaissance battalion reconnoiters up to a distance of about 60 miles (3 hours) ahead of the division over a front which should not exceed 40 miles.'

The 1942 Armoured Division Command Structure

The brigade-level command structure of the 1940 armoured division TO&E was done away with in the 1942 armoured division TO&E reorganization. In its place were two Combat Commands (CCs), the US Army's more formal equivalent of the German Army panzer division ad hoc *Kampfgruppen*.

Neither CC of the 1942 armoured division TO&E had in theory any organic units of their own but were intended to be the command elements for whatever mixture of battalions were attached to them for a specific mission set by the divisional headquarters. The bulk of an armoured division's tanks would be found in the two CCs.

From a US Army manual dated March 1942 titled *Armored Force Field Manual, Tactics and Technique* appears this extract on employment of the two CCs of the 1942 armoured division TO&E:

> In attack the combat command groups generally are disposed into four parts: a reconnaissance force (consisting of organic reconnaissance units and attack units), a striking force (the striking echelon consisting of tanks with engineers attached), a supporting force (consisting of the support echelon, i.e. the infantry, artillery, and tank destroyer units), and a reserve. Whether the striking force makes the initial attack or main attack will depend on the terrain and the extent and dispositions of the hostile anti-tank defenses.

Regrettably, in 1942 most US Army armour officers had yet to acquire the level of professional development desired to duplicate what their combat-experienced German panzer officer counterparts were practising with their *Kampfgruppen*. This led to many US Army armour officers preferring the much simpler functional separation of their battalions rather than embracing the combined-arms teams intended with the 1942 armoured division TO&E reorganization.

Beside the two CCs in the 1942 armoured division TO&E, there also existed a 'division reserve'. It consisted of various elements of the divisions; for example, infantry and artillery. It was not capable of independent action as it lacked a command element and remained under the direct orders of the divisional commander at all times. In addition, the single armoured infantry regiment of the 1942 armoured division TO&E was sometimes formed into a third CC by the 2nd and 3rd Armoured Divisions.

I Think We Can Do Better

No sooner had the manuals on the 1942 armoured division TO&E been released than there began another rethink on how to better organize the armoured divisions of the US Army. Everybody had an opinion but as McNair was chief of staff of the AGF it was his opinion that carried the most weight. McNair felt that the 1942 armoured division TO&E was still too large and cumbersome to be successful in battle. He wanted a much smaller and better-balanced armoured division TO&E arrangement with more infantry and artillery.

McNair believed that armoured divisions were only suitable for the 'exploitation role' and therefore should not make up more than 10 per cent of the US Army ground forces. His desire for much smaller armoured divisions was seconded by an organization convened between November 1942 and June 1943, referred to as the 'Reduction Board'.

The Reduction Board's officials quickly came to the decision that the 1942 armoured division TO&E was too large to be deployed overseas quickly and placed an unnecessary strain on the entire US Army logistical system. Between McNair and the Reduction Board a consensus was reached, which eventually led to another armoured division TO&E being approved in September 1943.

Devers was strongly opposed to the new 1943 armoured division TO&E. However, as he did not have oversight over the new armoured divisions being formed in the United States, he was powerless to stop them from being configured with the new armoured division TO&E. Devers did, however, preclude the overseas armoured divisions under his command, the 2nd and 3rd in the United Kingdom as well as the 1st Armoured Division in North Africa, from the conversion process.

The authorized personnel in the 1942 armoured division TO&E totalled 14,488, while the 1943 armoured division TO&E had an authorized personnel count of 10,936. To distinguish between the two types of armoured division TO&Es, those retaining the original 1942 TO&E were thereafter referred to unofficially as 'heavy' and those with the new 1943 TO&E were classified as 'light'.

The 1943 Armoured Division Structure

One of the most important changes in the 1943 armoured division TO&E was the elimination of regimental headquarters commands. In place of the two CCs in the heavy armoured division, the 1943 armoured division TO&E had three CCs that were normally referred to as 'CCA, CCB and CCR', with the letter 'R' standing for 'Reserve'. Like the other two CCs, it was capable of independent action if required. In theory, the CCR was always to be held in reserve by armoured divisions, but sometimes was fielded alongside the other CCs in the front lines by armoured divisional commanders.

The CCA and CCB of the 1943 armoured division TO&E each had approximately twelve officers and eighty enlisted men in their headquarters element. The CCR typically had only three officers and five enlisted men assigned as their headquarters element, reflecting its intended role as a non-tactical reserve. When converted into a fully-fledged CC, its headquarters element would be supplemented by assigning personnel from the divisional headquarters element.

The 1943 Armoured Division Components

The 1943 armoured division TO&E called for 245 tanks, consisting of 168 medium and 77 light variants. These were organized in three tank battalions, compared to the six tank battalions specified in the 1942 armoured division TO&E. Unlike the 1942 armoured division TO&E in which the medium tanks and light tanks were assigned to separate battalions, the 1943 TO&E called for a mix of medium and light tanks in all three battalions.

Each of the three tank battalions was subdivided into four companies, three of which were composed of medium tanks and one of light. The tank companies themselves were further subdivided into three platoons of five tanks each. The headquarters element of each of the three medium tank companies had an additional three medium tanks, one of which would be armed with a 105mm howitzer. The single light tank company in each tank battalion had only two tanks in its headquarters element, with no supporting howitzer-equipped tank.

Every tank company included a single fully-tracked medium tank recovery vehicle. In addition, each tank company had three trucks and a single half-track. Each battalion had a service company equipped with four tank recovery vehicles: two tracked and two wheeled. Besides a single half-track, the service company also had forty trucks of various sizes, many of which had trailers.

Overseeing each of the three tank battalions in the 1943 armoured division TO&E was a battalion headquarters and headquarters company equipped with five medium tanks, three of which were armed with 105mm howitzers. The two non-howitzer-equipped medium tanks were for the battalion commander and his operations officer. In some armoured divisions, all nine of the 105mm howitzer-equipped medium tanks in the medium tank companies' headquarters elements were attached to the armoured division artillery battalion.

There was also a mortar platoon in each tank battalion headquarters and headquarters company equipped with four mortar-equipped half-tracks. An additional seven half-tracks, eleven 0.25-ton 4 × 4 trucks (Jeeps) and a single 2.5-ton 6 × 6 truck made up the vehicle inventory of a tank battalion headquarters and headquarters company. These vehicles were divided between a battalion headquarters section, company headquarters, maintenance section, reconnaissance platoon and an ammunition and supply section.

More Details

It was not until the 1943 armoured division TO&E that medium tanks were mentioned as the main striking power of the division, with light tanks now playing a secondary role. This change can be seen in a US Army manual passage dated December 1944 and titled 'Tank Battalion':

> The light tanks may be used on reconnaissance and security missions. To feel out the enemy and develop weak spots in the enemy position for an attack by the medium tanks. To screen the advance of other tank units when enemy resistance is light or when the situation is vague … To protect the flanks of the medium tanks during the attack. When medium tanks are not available, to accompany infantry and assist its advance by destroying enemy positions. To assist the infantry in mopping-up.

The battalion of mechanized cavalry found in the 1942 armoured division TO&E was replaced by a smaller cavalry reconnaissance squadron (mechanized). Unlike the mechanized cavalry battalion of the 1942 armoured division TO&E that fought as individual units, the cavalry reconnaissance squadron (mechanized) of the 1943 armoured division TO&E typically allocated its reconnaissance troops to individual CCs as needed.

Besides the three tank battalions the 1943 armoured division TO&E had three armoured infantry battalions and three self-propelled armoured artillery battalions. The role of the latter is explained in this 15 August 1944 manual titled *Armored Division Artillery*:

> The primary mission of the armored field artillery is to provide close and continuous support to armored units by fire, neutralizing or destroying those targets which are most dangerous to the supported arm. In the progressive development of an action, it may support an advance guard or screening force, cover the assembly and development of the main body, deliver preparatory fires and fires in close support of the advance, and displace while rendering continuous close

> support. In the execution of these missions, the action may require armored field artillery to shift its fires in any direction against a threat to the flanks or rear, and to cover the rally of the tanks for purposes of refueling, resupplying ammunition, and reorganizing.

The 1943 armoured division TO&E called for a single maintenance, engineer and medical battalion. The organic bridge-laying company of the heavy armoured division engineer battalion was transferred to corps or army level control. However, it was then transferred back to the armoured divisions as an attachment.

Combat Command Structures

In theory, the three CCs of a 1943 armoured division TO&E had no organic fighting troops of their own unless allocated at the divisional level. The 4th Armoured Division was a strong believer in this arrangement and never assigned battalions to a CC on a fixed basis, preferring instead to retain a high degree of flexibility in its task organization. However, other armoured divisional commanders created CCs of fixed composition. This resulted in some 1943 TO&E armoured divisions giving each of their three CCs an equal number of tanks, infantry and artillery battalions. This type of organization with a CC was referred to as a 'balanced formation'.

Depending on the mission assigned, the CCs of an armoured division could be subdivided into smaller 'task forces' if required. Task forces normally consisted of mixed companies of tanks and infantry. They were typically named after the officer in command of the task force. One level down from the task force was the 'team'. These consisted of a mixed company of tanks and infantry. For example, a platoon of five tanks and forty infantrymen could act as a team. Teams were designated by a single capital letter such as Team A, B or C.

The Infantry Support Requirement

With the formation of the Armoured Force and the concentration of tanks in armoured divisions, the infantry branch was concerned that it would lack timely armour support when needed on the battlefield. In response, at the same time that the army's first two armoured divisions were stood up in July 1941, the first 'General Headquarters (GHQ) Tank Battalion' was formed. By the end of 1941 there were fifteen of these in existence and fourteen more were formed in 1942.

In March 1942, when the GHQ was relabelled as the 'Army Ground Forces' (AGF), the GHQ Tank Battalions were renamed 'Separate Tank Battalions'. By the end of 1943, there were seventy separate tank battalions. They would see service both in the ETO and the Pacific Theatre of Operation.

The separate tank battalions were never meant to be an organic part of an infantry division's TO&E. Rather, they remained under the Armoured Force/Armoured

Command and were intended to be allocated to infantry divisions to perform specific missions at army level discretion. Some in the US Army had already concluded at that time that a tank battalion should be organic to every infantry division.

If the need arose, separate tank battalions could also be employed to support armoured divisions, which rarely happened. From a 1945 US Army report is this passage summing up the employment of the separate tank battalions in the ETO:

> The Separate Tank Battalions were organized as GHQ Reserve Battalions, and were assigned to armies. However, in actual practice and operation, a tank battalion was attached to an infantry division and usually operated with it throughout the European campaign. But, because there were only twenty-eight medium and two light Separate Tank Battalions for forty-two infantry divisions in the theater, there were few that, for short periods, did not operate with two or more different divisions.

Due to the shortage of separate tank battalions in the ETO, it was common practice for self-propelled tank destroyer battalions to be attached to infantry divisions in lieu of the separate tank battalions. The tank destroyers had never been intended for this role as they were open-topped and therefore more vulnerable than tanks.

Despite the main purpose of the separate tank battalions being to work alongside infantry divisions, for the most part they received very little training in that role. This situation was noted by many army observers during the fighting in North Africa (1942–43) and later in Sicily (1943). In his 'Notes on Combat Experience during the Tunisian and African Campaign' Major General Ernest N. Harmon commented: 'We will not win this war with the tank alone, but we will not win the war without the tank … I have seen two enemy tanks practically annihilate a regiment of American infantry [without tank support] in 20 minutes.'

Compounding the problem with the separate tank battalions was the fact that those infantry officers in charge of them were never instructed in how to properly employ them in combat. To correct this problem a manual prepared by tank officers for their infantry counterparts was released in March 1944. Post-war, a tank battalion became organic to every US Army infantry division.

DR B3

(**Opposite, above**) Even as the Medium Tank M2A1 came off the production lines, it was clear to many that the tank's 37mm main gun and thin armour made it obsolete on the battlefields of Europe. This led to work beginning in June 1940 on a new medium tank design incorporating thicker armour and both a 37mm and 75mm guns. A year later that train of development led to the production of the M3 Medium Tank seen here. *(TACOM Historical Office)*

(**Opposite, below**) In this very dramatic staged shot taken at Fort Knox, Kentucky, we see the crew of this M3 medium tank pretending to abandon their vehicle and protect it with a wide variety of small-arms weapons, including pistols and submachine guns. Full-scale production of the M3 Medium Tank began in the summer of 1941 and continued until August 1942 with 5,000 units completed. *(Patton Museum)*

(**Above**) The construction of the M3 Medium Tank series began at the newly-built government-owned Detroit Arsenal Tank Plant. The plant was managed by Chrysler, as the company had the experience of mass production that the US Army lacked. Pictured here are a number of M3 Medium Tanks nearing completion on the factory floor. The 1942 armoured division (heavy) TO&E was authorized for 232 medium tanks. *(TACOM Historical Office)*

(**Above**) Completed M3 Medium Tanks are shown here being loaded on flatcars for delivery to the US Army at the Detroit Arsenal Tank Plant. Due to ever-increasing numbers of M3 Medium Tanks being ordered for both the US Army and various Allied nations under Lend-Lease, other companies besides Chrysler were brought in to build the M3 Medium Tank in different versions. *(TACOM Historical Office)*

(**Opposite, above**) A line illustration from a US Army manual lists the many components that made up the M3 Medium Tank. Due to the height of the air-cooled radial engine installed in the vehicle, its drive shaft to the front hull-mounted transmission was much higher than that of a comparable in-line or V-type engine. This in turn pushed up the height of the vehicle's hull and turret to 10ft 3in. *(US Army)*

(**Opposite, below**) The weight of this US Army M3 Medium Tank pictured during a training exercise in the United States in 1941 proved more than this bridge could support. The 1941 manoeuvres or war games were the largest ever held by the US Army. They were conducted to test its doctrine, organization and equipment in anticipation of going to war against the Axis Powers, especially Germany. *(National Archives)*

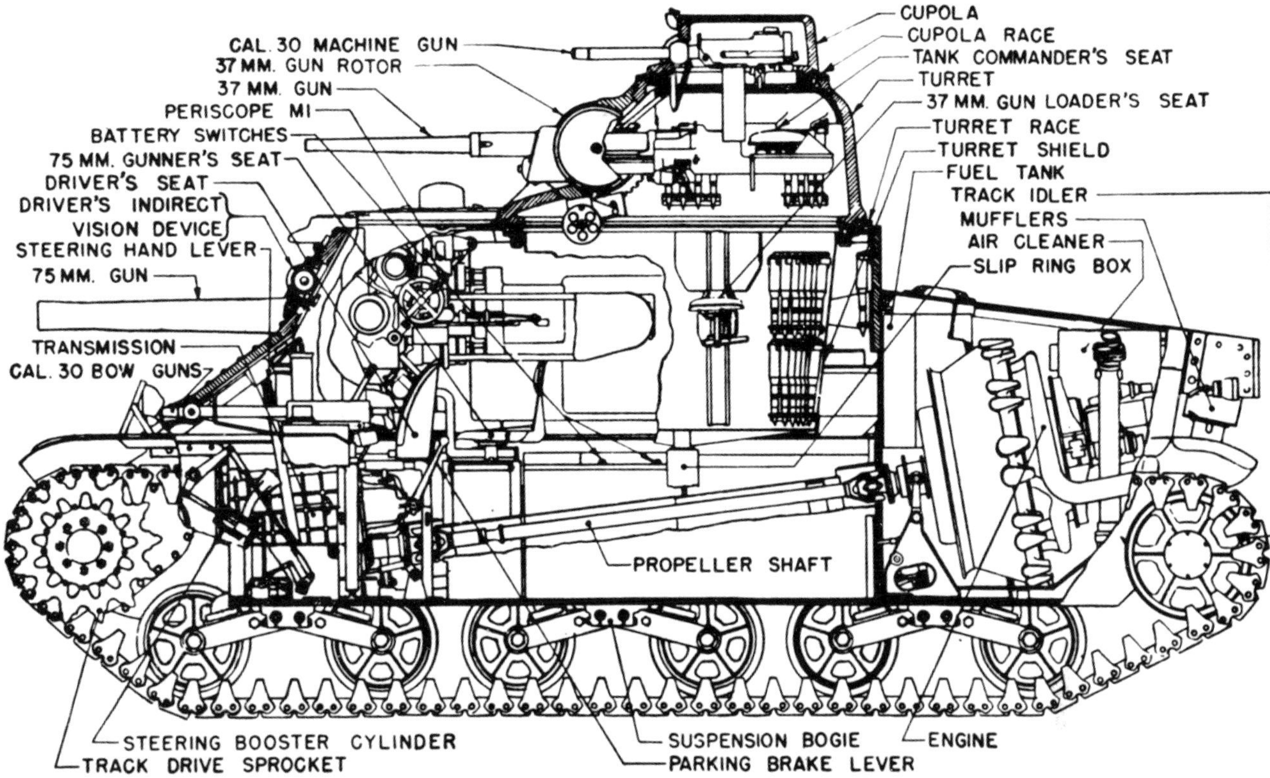
CUPOLA
CUPOLA RACE
TANK COMMANDER'S SEAT
TURRET
37 MM. GUN LOADER'S SEAT
TURRET RACE
TURRET SHIELD
FUEL TANK
TRACK IDLER
MUFFLERS
AIR CLEANER
SLIP RING BOX
CAL. 30 MACHINE GUN
37 MM. GUN ROTOR
37 MM. GUN
PERISCOPE MI
BATTERY SWITCHES
75 MM. GUNNER'S SEAT
DRIVER'S SEAT
DRIVER'S INDIRECT VISION DEVICE
STEERING HAND LEVER
75 MM. GUN
TRANSMISSION
CAL. 30 BOW GUNS
PROPELLER SHAFT
STEERING BOOSTER CYLINDER
TRACK DRIVE SPROCKET
SUSPENSION BOGIE
PARKING BRAKE LEVER
ENGINE

E-11-S-13

U.S.A. W-304433

(**Opposite, above**) Pictured at the US Army Desert Training Centre, established in April 1942, are a large number of M3 Medium Tanks. The centre encompassed an area that extended from the desert region of southern California into Western Arizona. The centre's first commander was Patton, who remained in that post until August 1942. *(National Archives)*

(**Opposite, below**) Late-production units of the M3 Medium Tank lacked the small escape hatches on either side of the upper hull as seen in this picture of a preserved example at a US Army museum. Those M3 Medium Tanks provided to the British Army had their machine-gun-armed vehicle commander's cupola removed and replaced with a two-piece overhead hatch as appears on the vehicle shown here. *(Chris Hughes)*

(**Above**) As with the early-production M3 Light Tank, the hull of the M3 Medium Tank was constructed of rolled homogenous armour plates riveted together as is clearly seen in this photograph. In contrast, the hull of the M2 and M2A1 Medium Tanks had been constructed of face-hardened armour plates riveted together. The front upper hull (glacis) plate on the M3 Medium Tank was 50mm thick. *(Author's collection)*

Lu Lu
Bell
-W-219241

(**Opposite, above**) In an effort to speed up production of the M3 Medium Tank, American industry came up with a cast-armour steel hull for the vehicle as seen here on this preserved example. In this configuration, the vehicle was designated the M3A1 Medium Tank, with only 300 units built between January and July 1942. Crew protection was also improved as rivets were known to shear off when riveted vehicles were struck by enemy fire. *(George Morrish)*

(**Opposite, below**) On 31 August 1940, the Armoured Force leadership released detailed characteristics for a desired new medium tank to be armed with a turret-mounted 75mm main gun. Busy with the M3 Medium Tank, the Ordnance Department had no time to begin work on the project until 1 February 1941. A wooden mock-up of the proposed new medium tank is pictured here in August 1941. *(Patton Museum)*

(**Above**) At the same time that the wooden mock-up of the new medium tank designated the T6 was ordered in June 1941, the Ordnance Committee ordered the building of a pilot version of the vehicle. That vehicle seen here rolled off the factory floor on 2 September 1941. It inherited the hull side escape hatches of the M3 Medium Tank as shown. *(Patton Museum)*

97

(**Opposite, above**) The T6 Medium Tank was standardized as the Medium Tank M4 on 5 September 1941. In December 1941, the Ordnance Committee decided that those built with a cast-armour upper hull (minus the hull escape hatches) would be designated the M4A1 Medium Tank and those with a welded-armour upper hull the M4 Medium Tank. Visible in this factory photograph are very early-production M4A1 Medium Tanks. *(TACOM Historical Office)*

(**Above**) Pictured here is an M4A1 Medium Tank. It has the very early-production direct-vision slots for the driver and bow machine-gunner but a later-production gun shield. Cast-armour upper hulls were cheaper and quicker to build than welded-armour upper hulls for the M4 Medium Tank series. Unfortunately, there was not enough foundry capacity to build as many M4A1 Medium Tanks as the US Army desired. *(Pierre-Olivier Buan)*

(**Opposite, below**) A derelict M4A1 with the early-production cast-armor gun shield. The first cast-armour-hull M4A1 came off the assembly line in February 1942. Production of the cast-armour M4A1 took place at three factories and continued until December 1943, with 6,281 units built. It rode on a vertical volute spring suspension (VVSS) system as had first appeared on the T5 Light Tank in 1934. *(Pierre-Olivier Buan)*

(**Above**) On display in France is this M4 Medium Tank with the upper welded hull. Production of this version began in July 1942. By the time production of the tank concluded in January 1944, a total of 6,748 units had been completed. Both the M4 and the M4A1 Medium Tank were powered by air-cooled, gasoline-powered radial engines. The M4 and M4A1 formed the mainstay of the US Army armoured divisions in the ETO until the late summer of 1944. *(Pierre-Olivier Buan)*

(**Opposite, above**) In this photograph we can see two early-production M4 series Medium Tanks side-by-side. Both have the direct-vision slots in the front hull and the original narrow gun shield for their 75mm main guns. The M4 Medium Tank on the left is riding on all-steel tracks and the M4 Medium Tank on the right the Ordnance Department-developed double-pinned, rubber-blocked tracks that had first appeared on the T2E1 Light Tank in early 1935. *(Patton Museum)*

(**Opposite, below**) The air-cooled, gasoline-powered radial engines of the M4 and M4A1 Medium Tanks were not the perfect choice as a tank power plant but were all that was available at the time. When the Ford Motor Company was brought into production of the M4 series tanks in August 1941, the company offered an in-house-designed, liquid-cooled, gasoline-powered V-8 engine that they referred to as the 'GAA'. Installed in a welded-hull model as seen here, it was designated the M4A3 Medium Tank. *(Author's collection)*

5
34-H-5
34-I-13

35
C-6

(**Above**) Seen here is an M4A3 Medium Tank. The external appearance of the tank was almost identical to that of the M4 Medium Tank. The only major difference between them was the configuration of their respective rear-hull engine compartments. A total of 1,690 units of the M4A3 were built between June 1942 and September 1943. Due to the superiority of its engine it was the preferred tank of the US Army armoured divisions beginning in the late summer of 1944. *(Pierre-Olivier Buan)*

(**Opposite, above**) The replacement for the M3 series Light Tanks in US Army armoured divisions was the M5 Light Tank. Its most noticeable design feature seen on this preserved example is its sloped upper-hull plate, which was 29mm thick. By moving the front hull plate forward, there was now more room for the driver and the bow-gunner and the provision for front hull overhead hatches. *(Pierre-Olivier Buan)*

(**Opposite, below**) The small two-man turret of the M5 Light Tank was the same as found on the M3A1 Light Tank. The biggest external difference between the two light tanks was the greatly-enlarged rear engine compartment of the M5 seen here as it was powered by two liquid-cooled, gasoline-powered Cadillac car engines. Production of the M5 Light Tank began in April 1942 and continued until December 1942, with 2,074 units constructed. *(Author's collection)*

2
16
3Δ-13
G-13

U.S.A.
W 3044280

USA
3051298
F-12

USA
3047787
FISH 'N CHIPS

(**Opposite, above**) A progressively-improved version of the M5 Light Tank was the M5A1 Light Tank pictured here. The most noticeable external difference between it and its predecessor was the new turret design that featured a bustle for mounting a radio. The M5A1's turret came from the M3A3 Light Tank, which was never used by the US Army but reserved for Lend-Lease. *(Chun-lun Hsu)*

(**Opposite, below**) Late-production units of the M5A1 Light Tank, an example of which is pictured here, can be identified by the enclosed curved storage box attached to the right-hand side of its turret. This was for the storage of a .30 calibre machine gun. The 1942 armoured division TO&E was authorized 158 light tanks. In the 1943 armoured division TO&E there were only eighty-three light tanks authorized. *(Author's collection)*

(**Above**) In August 1942, the Ordnance Department met with the senior leadership of the Armoured Force to decide on the next generation of light tanks to replace the already obsolete M3 and M5 series Light Tanks. The eventual result was the fielding of the four-man M24 Light Tank seen here. *(Pierre-Olivier Buan)*

USA
W403298

MAX. SPEED
30 M.P.H.
NO SIGNAL

(**Opposite, above**) In desperate need of a vehicle for the armoured infantry units of the newly-formed armoured divisions, in September 1940 the Ordnance Department standardized three different models of an open-topped, armoured Half-Track Car T14 and authorized their production. The version pictured here is the Half-Track Car M2. The 1942 armoured division TO&E was authorized 163 units. *(Patton Museum)*

(**Opposite, below**) Among the three versions of the Half-Track Car T14 authorized for production in September 1940 was the Half-Track Personnel Carrier M3 seen here. It was a lengthened version of the Half-Track Car M2 and could transport thirteen men. The 1942 armoured division TO&E called for a total of 441 units of the Half-Track Personnel Carrier M3. *(Pierre-Olivier Buan)*

(**Above**) Shown here is an M3A1 Half-Track Personnel Carrier. The big difference between it and its predecessor the M3 was the ring mount on the right front of the vehicle, armed with a .50 calibre machine gun. The 1943 armoured division TO&E was authorized 448 of the M3 series half-track with 216 units divided among its three armoured infantry battalions. *(Christophe Vallier)*

The eventual replacement for the Half-Track Car M3A1 was the Light Armoured Car M8 seen here. The 1942 armoured division TO&E called for seventy-five units of the M8 located in the armoured reconnaissance battalion. The 1943 armoured division TO&E was authorized fifty-four units of the M8 in their cavalry reconnaissance squadron (Mechanized). *(Christophe Vallier)*

Another variant of the Light Armoured Car M8 employed by the US Army's armoured divisions was the version seen here labelled the Armoured Utility Car M20. In the 1943 armoured division TO&E there was a single M20 assigned to the divisional artillery commander. The self-propelled tank destroyer battalions attached to armoured divisions had thirty of the M20s authorized. *(Pierre-Olivier Buan)*

Seen here is five-star general of the US Army George C. Marshall, Jr. Post-First World War he became aide-de-camp to General John J. Pershing who was appointed as the US Army chief of staff following the conflict. Marshall became the US Army chief of staff in 1939. It was he who authorized the formation of the Armoured Force on 10 June 1940. (*National Archives*)

Pictured together during the 1941 Louisiana Manoeuvres are Lieutenant General Lesley J. McNair on the right and Major General Omar Bradley on the left. Marshall stated that McNair was 'the brains of the US Army' and had placed him in charge of the General Headquarters, United States Army (GHQ) in July 1940, which was responsible for equipping and training the army. (*National Archives*)

Brigadier General George S. Patton is seen here during the Louisiana Manoeuvres, which were conducted between August and September 1941. He had been assigned command of the 2nd Armoured Division in April 1941. On the last day of the Louisiana Manoeuvres, Patton and fellow like-minded officers began to discuss how to create a mechanized force independent of both the cavalry and infantry branches. *(Patton Museum)*

(**Opposite, above**) In this picture taken during the summer war games of 1941 we see Patton standing inside an M3A1 Scout Car along with then Lieutenant Colonel Robert W. Grow, who as a major general would command the 6th Armoured Division. Patton is wearing a tanker's helmet of his own design. He was nicknamed the 'Green Hornet' after a well-known comic book and radio character of the time, due to his habit of mounting sirens on his command vehicles. *(Patton Museum)*

(**Opposite, below left**) If anybody can be considered the founder of the Armoured Force, it was Adna R. Chaffee. Sadly, after being stricken with cancer, he would die on 22 August 1941. The day before his death, command of the Armoured Force passed to the very able leadership of Jacob L. Devers, seen here as a four-star general. It was Devers who pushed for the development of the M4 series of medium tanks. He left the post of Armoured Force commander in May 1943 to take a higher-level position. *(National Archives)*

(**Opposite, below right**) Upon Devers' departure as Armoured Force commander, the position was filled by Alvan Gillem seen here, who eventually rose to the rank of lieutenant general. Unlike Devers, who would often clash with McNair over the organization and equipment of the Armoured Force, Gillem tended to defer to McNair, which led to the Armoured Force having much less clout and influence that it had had under Chaffee and Devers. *(Patton Museum)*

(**Opposite, above**) The brainchild of McNair was the 'Tank Destroyer Force', which he saw as the most effective counter to enemy mass tank attacks. The initial problem for the Tank Destroyer Force was the lack of any suitable equipment. As a stopgap they fielded the 37mm gun motor carriage (GMC) M6 pictured here. The vehicle was also found in the 1942 armoured division (heavy) but not in the 1943 armoured division (light) TO&E. *(Patton Museum)*

(**Opposite, below**) The second ad hoc tank destroyer fielded was the half-track 75mm Gun Motor Carriage (GMC) seen here. It consisted of the Half-Track Personnel Carrier M3 modified to mount a First World War-vintage 75mm field gun. Production of the 75mm GMC M3 began in February 1942 and ended in February 1943, with a total of 2,116 units completed. *(Don Moriarty)*

(**Above**) Based on the M4A2 Medium Tank chassis was the 3-inch Gun Motor Carriage M10 seen here. It was in production between September 1942 and December 1943, with a total of 4,993 units assembled. When ordered into production it had a higher order of priority than the M4 Medium Tank series. Another 1,713 units were based on the chassis of the M4A3 Medium Tank and labelled the M10A1. *(Pierre-Olivier Buan)*

USA
40177445-S
A
12

(**Opposite, above**) The Tank Destroyer Force considered the M10/M10A1 an expedient vehicle forced upon them by the Ordnance Department and McNair. The one vehicle that was supposed to be the ideal tank destroyer was the 76mm Gun Motor Carriage M18 seen here, which first came off the Buick Motor Division assembly lines of General Motors in July 1943. It was often found in late-war tank destroyer battalions attached to armoured divisions. *(Pierre-Olivier Buan)*

(**Opposite, below**) In anticipation of the German Army fielding more heavily-armoured tanks that would be impervious to the guns on the M18 and M10/M10A1 tank destroyers, the Ordnance Department standardized the 90mm Gun Motor Carriage (GMC) M36 tank destroyer seen here in July 1944. Initial arrival of the M36 in the ETO took place in August 1944. *(Pierre-Olivier Buan)*

(**Above**) The US Army had a strong pre-war interest in self-propelled artillery pieces but funding shortfalls made that impossible to pursue. When the Second World War began on 1 September 1939, its only mechanized artillery units existed in the 1st Cavalry (Mechanized) Battalion. They employed 6 × 6 trucks towing the modernized First World War M1897 75mm gun pictured here. *(Pierre-Olivier Buan)*

(**Above**) When production caught up with demand, the 1940 armoured divisions depended on the new M2 Half-Track Car to tow the 105mm howitzer seen here until such time as a 105mm self-propelled howitzer could be fielded. In its original form the 105mm towed howitzer was designated the M2. It later became the improved M2A1 seen here. *(Pierre-Olivier Buan)*

(**Opposite, above**) The first self-propelled artillery piece found in the 1942 armoured division (heavy) was the half-track 105mm Howitzer Motor Carriage (HMC) T19 pictured here. It entered into service in January 1942 and was developed as a stopgap until a fully-tracked vehicle armed with a 105mm howitzer could be developed. There were fifty-four authorized in the 1942 armoured division (heavy) TO&E. *(Patton Museum)*

(**Opposite, below**) The successful fielding of the half-track 105mm Howitzer Motor Carriage (HMC) T19 led the Ordnance Department to authorize for the Armoured Force the development of the 75mm Howitzer Motor Carriage (HMC) T30 pictured here. Based on the modified chassis of the Half-Track Personnel Carrier M3, there were forty-two authorized in the 1942 armoured division (heavy) TO&E. *(Patton Museum)*

HAIRBREDTH

(**Above**) The eventual replacement for the half-track-based 105mm Howitzer Motor Carriage (HMC) T19 within armoured divisions was the half-track-based 105mm Howitzer Motor Carriage (HMC) M7 series, an example of which is seen here. Both the 1942 armoured division (heavy) TO&E and that of the 1943 armoured division (light) were authorized fifty-four units of the M7 HMC series. *(Author's collection)*

(**Opposite, above**) Standardized in May 1942 was the 75mm Howitzer Motor Carriage (HMC) M8 pictured here. It was based on the modified chassis of the Light Tank M5 and was the replacement for the half-track-based 75mm Howitzer Motor Carriage (HMC) T30. The 1943 armoured division (light) TO&E was authorized eleven units of the M8 HMC, with eight in the division's reconnaissance squadron. *(Chris Hughes)*

(**Opposite, below**) As soon as the M4 series of tanks was envisioned, a 105mm howitzer-armed version was intended to be built for the Armoured Command. That vehicle did not come to fruition until February 1944, based on both the M4 and M4A3 second-generation models, the former being labelled the M4(105) and the latter the M4A3(105). Pictured here is an M4(105). *(Pierre-Olivier Buan)*

13
T212125
COUGAR

TENEZ BON
NOUS
ARRIVONS

(**Opposite, above**) As early as June 1941 the Ordnance Department began studying the possibility of mounting a 155mm gun on a modified chassis of an M3 Medium Tank. Testing of the pilot showed that its mobility was far superior to that of its towed counterpart. It was therefore decided to standardize it as the 155mm Gun Motor Carriage (GMC) M12 seen here. *(Patton Museum)*

(**Opposite, below**) Each 1943 armoured division (light) TO&E was assigned eight L4-H single-engine liaison aircraft, an example of which is seen here. Two were found in the division headquarters company, with two more assigned to each of the division's three artillery battalions. Besides liaison duties, the two-man aircraft were also employed in the artillery observation role. *(Pierre-Olivier Buan)*

(**Above**) Pictured here is a Dodge WC 6.5-ton 4 × 4 Command and Reconnaissance Car, which was first in US Army service in the early 1930s. It had provisions for a radio and antenna. With a winch, it became the WC-7. There were a map-holder and folding table located on the rear side of the front seat. The same chassis came in a number of different configurations. *(Author's collection)*

(**Above**) During the Second World War the Harley-Davidson motorcycle pictured here was labelled the 'chain drive solo motorcycle'. There were 192 units found in the 1942 armoured division (heavy) TO&E. With the introduction of the far superior 0.25-ton 4 x 4 truck (Jeep), they were all taken out of service. Motorcycles were never part of the 1943 armoured division (light) TO&E. *(Chris Hughes)*

(**Opposite, above**) The 0.25-ton 4 x 4 truck seen here weighed 3,253lb and was originally developed by the Quartermaster Corps. However, the responsibility for its continued development was transferred to the Ordnance Department in August 1942. The vehicle had several nicknames including 'Jeep', 'peep' and 'Bantam'. There were 550 authorized for the 1942 armoured division TO&E and 451 for the 1943 armoured division TO&E. *(Chris Hughes)*

(**Opposite, below**) The 1942 armoured division TO&E called for fifty-one units of the 0.75-ton 4 x 4 Weapon Carrier seen here. Built by Dodge, it was assigned the company designation WC-51, or WC-52 if it came with a winch. Sixteen were located in the division's service company, three in the signal company and twenty-nine in the division's train. The 1943 armoured division TO&E had only twenty-seven units of the Weapon Carrier. *(Christophe Vallier)*

U.S.A.
20387132
S

USA

3504317
PRESTONE 42
NM
H 014
87-336
HQ-9

78342

(**Opposite, above**) A lengthened version of the Dodge WC-51 0.75-ton 4 × 4 Weapon Carrier is the Dodge WC-62 1.5-ton 6 × 6 cargo truck seen here. With a winch, the company labelled it the WC-63. It was intended as a substitute for the GMC-built 2.5-ton 6 × 6 cargo truck when the latter was not available in sufficient numbers. It could be found in tank destroyer battalions, typically attached to armoured divisions. *(Christophe Vallier)*

(**Opposite, below**) Based on the chassis of the Dodge 0.75-ton 4 × 4 weapon carrier truck is the Dodge WC-61 0.75-ton 4 × 4 Emergency Repair truck seen here. To support the body's extra weight, it has dual rear wheels. The 1942 armoured division (heavy) was authorized seventy-nine repair trucks of various sizes and configurations. The 1943 armoured division (light) TO&E had only thirty-one repair trucks authorized. *(Christophe Vallier)*

(**Above**) A total of 29,502 units were built of the Dodge Truck, 0.75-ton 4 × 4 Ambulance seen here, labelled by the company as the WC-54. It used a longer body than the WC-51 and others. The 1942 armoured division (heavy) had a total of forty units, while the 1943 armoured division (light) had thirty authorized. Like the other eleven models in the Dodge G-502 series, they had a maximum speed on level roads of 54mph. *(Christophe Vallier)*

275750 USA
USA
126864
WSU
806
HQ7

(**Opposite, above**) The 1942 armoured division (heavy) TO&E authorized sixteen sedans for high-ranking officers. All were pre-war standard 4 × 2 civilian cars painted in olive drab and equipped with blackout light equipment. The example pictured here is a Chrysler Royal Sedan, which would be considered a light sedan. A larger and roomier model built by Packard was referred to as a medium sedan. *(Christophe Vallier)*

(**Opposite, below**) To recover the vehicles of the armoured divisions there was the M1 Heavy Wrecker 6-ton 6 × 6 seen here. The 1942 armoured division (heavy) had a total of thirty-nine units, while the 1943 armoured division (light) had only eleven. In both types of armoured divisions, the majority of the M1 heavy wrecking trucks were located in the divisional maintenance battalions. *(Author's collection)*

(**Above**) For recovering the tanks of the 1943 armoured division (light) there were twenty-four units of the M31 series tank recovery vehicle, an example of which is pictured here. They were based on various models of the M3 Medium Tank series. To disguise its purpose on the battlefield it had a dummy 75mm gun barrel in the front hull. A total of 805 units of the M31 series tank recovery vehicles were built. *(Andreas Kirchhoff)*

USA
30103986

U.S.A. 545620
1△920RD
D17

(**Opposite, above**) The replacement for the M31 series tank recovery vehicle was the M32 series of tank recovery vehicles based on various versions of the M4 series of medium tanks. Besides the A-frame lifting boom seen erected in this museum diorama, the vehicle came with a 60,000lb capacity winch installed on the hull floor behind the driver. *(Pierre-Olivier Buan)*

(**Opposite, below**) One of the most impressive and largest vehicles in the 1943 armoured division (light) was the armoured M26 Heavy Tractor Truck seen here with the M15A1 trailer. The combination of the tractor truck and trailer was nicknamed the 'Dragon Wagon'. A subsequent version of the M26 tractor truck was unarmoured and open-topped and labelled the M26A1. *(Author's collection)*

(**Above**) The 1942 armoured division TO&E was authorized sixty-eight units of the 37mm gun M3A1 pictured here. All were towed into action by the M2 half-track car. Obsolete by the time of Operation TORCH (November 1942), they were all that was available. Thirty-seven were found in the armoured infantry regiment, twenty-seven in the armoured engineer battalion and three in the division train. *(Pierre-Olivier Buan)*

(**Above**) Found in the 1943 armoured division TO&E were thirty units of the towed 57mm gun M1, an example of which is seen here. They were located in the three armoured infantry battalions of the division, with each of the three companies of the armoured infantry battalions having an anti-tank platoon of three 57mm guns towed by the M2A1 half-track car. *(Chris Hughes)*

(**Opposite, above**) The second most numerous vehicle in both the 1942 and 1943 armoured division TO&E was the 2.5-ton 6 × 6 cargo truck seen here. Nicknamed the 'deuce and a half', approximately 560,000 units were built by General Motors Corporation (GMC), with the firm labelling it the CCKW. The 1942 armoured division TO&E called for 823 units and the 1943 armoured division TO&E 426 units. *(Christophe Vallier)*

(**Opposite, below**) The 1942 armoured division TO&E had a single armoured engineer battalion. It was subdivided into three engineer companies. Each company had a single 6 × 6 bridge-erecting truck seen here carrying a bridge section. For lifting off the bridge section the truck was fitted with a rear-mounted hydraulically-operated derrick, pictured here in its stowed position. *(Pierre-Olivier Buan)*

Trouble
8
814
XUL

5A-
22E
HQ-
14

Not normally part of the TO&E for either the 1942 or 1943 armoured divisions, the non-amphibious M28 Cargo Carrier seen here and an improved amphibious version designated the M29 and M29C Cargo Carriers (not pictured) were provided to armoured divisions when weather and terrain conditions prevented the use of other vehicles such as the 0.25-ton 4 × 4 truck (Jeep). *(Christophe Vallier)*

Chapter Three

Into the Fray

The combat initiation of the US Army's first two armoured divisions took place on 8 November 1942 during Operation TORCH, the Anglo-American invasion of Vichy-controlled French North Africa. The US Army committed CCB of the 1st Armoured Division and elements of the 2nd Armoured Division to the invasion force, which included six separate tank battalions. They were organized under the 1st and 2nd Tank Groups, each of which was assigned three of the separate tank battalions.

Overall command of all the armour units involved in Operation TORCH, which lasted from 8 to 16 November 1942, was assigned to the 1st Armoured Corps, which was reactivated for the invasion of French North Africa. The 1st Armoured Corps was given the cover name 'Western Task Force' and was under the command of Patton.

The 2nd Armoured Division was the main striking power of the 1st Armoured Corps and tasked with the mission of securing French Morocco. CCB of the 1st Armoured Division was the main striking force of the 'Centre Task Force' and was assigned six separate tank battalions of the 1st and 2nd Tank Groups to aid in its seizure of French Algeria.

A Quick Victory

As the Vichy (pro-German) French government officials in Morocco and Algeria had little hope of stopping the invading Anglo-American forces, they quickly signed an armistice on 11 November 1942, which brought an end to all fighting. The three days of combat cost approximately 1,200 Allied dead and wounded, and about 3,000 Vichy French dead and wounded.

There were only two combat engagements between small numbers of tanks from the 1st and 2nd Armoured Divisions and those of Vichy French forces. Both occurred on 9 November 1942 and resulted in the French armour units being defeated. As US Army armoured divisions were supposed to concentrate on the exploitation role with tank destroyers taking care of enemy tanks, almost no guidance had been provided to the officers and men of the armoured battalions on how to even deal with enemy tanks.

The Big Picture

Even before French Morocco and Algeria were secured, the British First Army, along with CCB of the 1st Armoured Division, was sent racing eastward to French Tunisia. It was hoped that they could secure it before the Germans could take control from the local Vichy French forces. Despite their best efforts, the British and American forces were beaten by the Germans. This resulted in a stalemate with both sides involved in a race to build up their respective forces in French Tunisia for further offensive operations.

The Anglo-American plans called for the campaign to seize all of French Tunisia to begin in March 1943, with the US Army divisions in theatre playing only a defensive role. The German Army did not wait for that to happen and made plans to launch their own offensive operations. By early January 1943, the German commander of Tunisia had amassed a force of 45,000 men, including 15,000 Italian soldiers. There were approximately 200 German tanks and a much smaller number of Italian tanks on hand.

The late-arriving units of the 1st Armoured Division arrived in French Tunisia in January 1943, giving it a grand total of approximately 300 light and medium tanks. The division was commanded by Major General Orlando Ward and was the most powerful part of the US Army II Corps, which was under the command of Lieutenant General Lloyd Fredendall. The US Army II Corps reported to the First British Army led by Lieutenant General Kenneth Anderson. He in turn reported to Eisenhower, the supreme commander of all the Allied forces in the Mediterranean.

Despite its impressive strength on paper, the 1st Armoured Division had been unable to take part in any large-scale training exercises for the eleven months prior to its arrival in French North Africa as it was in transit from the United States to overseas. This left its personnel badly undertrained in their ability to effectively employ the division's weapons and equipment on the battlefield. What training manuals it had were already out of date regarding the realities of modern combined-arms combat. The US Army's newest Armoured Force manuals that came out in the latter part of 1942 which better reflected a more modern combat doctrine never reached the 1st or 2nd Armoured Divisions overseas.

The 2nd Armoured Division was not deployed to French Tunisia for a couple of reasons: it could not be supported logistically from the US Army supply bases in French Morocco, and initially served as a reserve force in case of possible German attacks on French Morocco through Spain. It therefore remained in French Algeria under Patton's 1st Armoured Corps along with two separate tank battalions.

As any possible threat of a German attack through Spain eventually waned, those US Army armoured units in French Morocco began training in preparation for the planned invasion of the island of Sicily. This proved difficult as personnel and equipment were continually stripped from them to keep the 1st Armoured Division up to full strength during the fierce fighting in French Tunisia.

The Fighting Begins

A series of sparring matches between the 1st Armoured Division and the German panzer divisions in French Tunisia began in early December 1942 and continued until 18 February 1943. The initial engagement between the American tankers in French Tunisia and their German counterparts occurred on 10 December 1942 when CCB of the 1st Armoured Division attempted to pull back from a battle. Its reconnaissance elements had failed to reconnoitre the withdrawal route so blundered into an impassable area and lost 18 tanks and 132 other vehicles.

The German intention from December 1942 through to February 1943, which they accomplished, was to push the US Army II Corps back to the Atlas Mountains in central Tunisia and away from the open plains of eastern Tunisia where it could threaten their supply lines. The US Army II Corps withdrawal left them to defend several narrow mountain passes to prevent the German panzer divisions advancing further westward.

As the German leadership saw the line defended by the US Army II Corps in Tunisia as a weak spot, they decided on a major offensive operation aimed at pushing through the mountain passes defended by the Americans. That offensive began on 19 February 1943 in a series of engagements that ran through to 26 February. It was collectively named after one of the American-defended mountain passes as the 'Battle for Kasserine Pass'.

By the time the Battle for Kasserine Pass concluded, the 1st Armoured Division had taken a serious drubbing from two German panzer divisions. The division lost more than 100 tanks and thousands of men killed, wounded and captured in what Ernie Pyle (famous American wartime journalist) described as a 'damned humiliating rout' on 19 and 20 February.

In spite of these losses, the 1st Armoured Division and US Army II Corps quickly pulled themselves together and managed to halt the German advance, which had outrun its supply lines. They then launched a counter-attack on 22 February 1943 that recaptured all the ground the Germans had taken. The key player in bringing the German advance to a halt and the resulting American counter-offensive was the overwhelming effectiveness of US Army artillery fire.

In Retrospect

The numerous mistakes that led to the poor showing of the 1st Armoured Division during the initial stages of the Battle for Kasserine Pass cannot be blamed solely on the division and its men. It was Fredendall and those above him that decided the lines in Tunisia held by the US Army II Corps were an inactive area. Therefore there were an unheard-of four CCs being formed from the 1st Armoured Division's assets: CCA, CCB, CCC and CCD.

The four CCs of the 1st Armoured Division were spread out over a wide area in a defensive posture and some were not even under the division's control. This was a complete rejection of the then accepted doctrine that armoured division resources needed to be massed and used primarily for exploitation. Eisenhower had spotted this doctrinal mistake before the Battle for Kasserine Pass and had told Fredendall to place the 1st Armoured Division into operational reserve as a counter to any German attacks, but time ran out before this could be implemented as there were no infantry divisions to take its place.

The Armoured Force/Armoured Command itself can be blamed for some of the difficulties experienced by the 1st Armoured Division at Kasserine Pass. It had an obsolete doctrine in place. Another serious issue that plagued the 1st Armoured Division at Kasserine Pass was the fact that the Armoured Force/Armoured Command had still not emphasized the practice of combined-arms warfare in the structure of its CCs.

After-Action Comments

Following the surrender of all German and Italian forces in North Africa in May 1943, a review began of what had worked and not worked for the 1st Armoured Division in the French North African campaign. In an after-action report titled 'Tankers in Tunisia' complied at Fort Knox in July 1943 from oral interviews conducted in theatre appeared a number of interesting quotes. One of these came from Sergeant Neal of the 1st Armoured Division:

> What I've learned here in Africa is that it is important to respect, not fear, the [German] 88mm guns. You must keep in turret defilade. They can knock you out at 3,000 yards. I have also learned that tanks must have support. If we had air and infantry, we could have done a good job. If the infantry had been ahead of us at Pass, they could have helped quite a bit.

In a number of post-operation memos among senior US Army officers, including Devers, the Armoured Force commander until May 1943, and Marshall, there were serious evaluations of the 1st Armoured Division's performance during the fighting in North Africa. These are seen in a passage from a book titled *Mobility, Shock and Firepower: The Emergence of the US Army's Armor Branch, 1917–1945* by Robert S. Cameron:

> Errors made during maneuvers [1940–41] recurred in battle. Armored units ignored the use of concealment and deception. They routinely conducted frontal assaults rather than employ flanking maneuvers. They also failed to effectively coordinate the action of infantry, artillery, and tanks. Tank crews

demonstrated a propensity for rapid, wild fire that rapidly exhausted ammunition and gave away their location with little effect on the enemy. Neglect of fire and movement principles led one 1st Armored Division officer to conclude: 'These matters have been drilled into our troops repeatedly for two years but apparently, it takes enemy bullets to make this lesson stick.'

Despite the damage inflicted on the 1st Armoured Division at the Battle for Kasserine Pass, it was a learning experience for the division as seen in this passage from a US Army Centre for Military History monograph titled 'Tunisia':

> Greater success with [American] armor came when panzer tactics were adopted: a deliberate tank-infantry advance preceded by intensive reconnaissance and heavy artillery. In the latter stages of the campaign [for French Tunisia] a formula was laid down: one tank battalion in the attack should have three artillery battalions in support.

Post-Battle Thoughts

Devers was well aware that the 1st Armoured Division's poor showing in Tunisia provided ammunition for McNair's efforts to shrink the size of the existing 1942 TO&E. He therefore instructed the new division commander, Major General Ernest N. Harmon, on a visit by McNair in theatre: 'You and your officers should have a great influence when McNair visits you and I hope that you can convince him that he is on the wrong track when he cuts men and vehicles so thin that the unit cannot operate.'

Major General Alvan C. Gillem (from the infantry branch), who replaced Devers as Armoured Force commander in May 1943, made a visit to French Tunisia and in August 1943 sent a report to McNair. In that report he mentioned one of the serious issues that had become apparent to him. In spite of the training centre at Fort Knox providing a sufficient number of qualified enlisted personnel for both tank and reconnaissance units, on arrival in theatre they were being diverted to other jobs for which they had not been trained; however, the reverse of that was also taking place. Those with no training in armour and reconnaissance were reassigned to armour units.

Some Suggestions Are Applied

Devers was not unaware that the fighting in French Tunisia had plainly indicated that there were some flaws with the 1942 Armoured Division TO&E. One of these was the retention of a regimental headquarters, inherited from the 1940 armoured division TO&E. It unnecessarily complicated the chain of command between the divisional commander and the battalion commanders of the Combat Commands when prompt action was required. The 1st Armoured Division's chief of staff decided 'It would appear desirable to eliminate either the regimental [headquarters] echelon or the combat command [headquarters] echelon to secure increased speed and execution of orders.'

There was another suggestion to improve its combat effectiveness made by the now combat-experienced officers of the 1st Armoured Division in French Tunisia. It proposed the transfer of the supply, maintenance and reconnaissance elements overseen by the regimental headquarters down to the tank and infantry battalion level. The officers felt that such a change in the division's TO&E would speed up the reaction time of CC commanders on the battlefield who would no longer have to devote time consulting with their regimental headquarters level about their decisions. These suggestions and others were taken up by McNair, who eliminated the regimental echelon with the 1943 armoured division TO&E in September 1943.

Sicilian Invasion

With the surrender of all Axis forces in Tunisia in May 1943, Anglo-American preparations to seize the island of Sicily, code-named Operation HUSKY, began in earnest. This time around the 1st Armoured Division would remain in Tunisia to be refitted for the eventual invasion of Italy, while the 2nd Armoured Division conducted the invasion of Sicily. The 2nd Armoured Division would be part of the Seventh Army under Patton during the Sicilian campaign. The 1st Armoured Corps was deactivated for the last time as the American invasion fleet headed to Sicily.

The Anglo-American armies' initial landings took place on the morning of 10 July 1943. The 2nd Armoured Division, commanded by Major General Hugh J. Gaffey, was to remain on its transport ships as a floating reserve to commit when needed. Patton ordered elements of the division ashore on the afternoon of 10 July 1943. Unfortunately, due to the weather and poor beach conditions, it took the division until nightfall of 11 July 1943 before it had a credible portion of its assets ashore. The 2nd Armoured Division did fight off German armoured counter-attacks, with crucial support from Allied naval gunfire.

As the topography of Sicily was extremely rugged with a very limited road network, there was little call for the employment of the 2nd Armoured Division after the initial landings. It spent a great deal of its time in reserve so that when an offensive opportunity arose it could respond quickly. The only time this occurred was when the division made a 100-mile dash in six days from the city of Agrigento, captured on 17 July 1943, to Palermo, the largest city on the island. The division, under Patton, was carrying out a plan to try to seize the port city of Messina to block German units attempting to flee from Sicily to the Italian mainland. Sicily was secured by the Allies on 17 August 1943.

The Italian Campaign

The American Fifth Army, under the command of Lieutenant General Mark Clark, had put its first infantry divisions and their separate tank battalions ashore on the Italian mainland at Salerno on 9 September 1943. As Italy's topography, especially the western portion assigned to the American Fifth Army, was much like Sicily, there was little anticipation of conducting large-scale offensive armoured operations. This resulted in only the 1st Armoured Division being assigned to the theatre.

The initial elements of the 1st Armoured Division began arriving in Italy in October 1943. The division had enough assets on hand by the end of 1943 to form CCB. The first major offensive operation involving CCB was during the Battle of Monte Cassino, which began on 17 January 1944 and ran through to May of that year. Coming up against strong German defences, rugged terrain and poor weather conditions, there were no breakthroughs of German lines that would allow CCB of the 1st Armoured Division to take up offensive operations.

To place more pressure on the German defences at Monte Cassino, the American Fifth Army, along with British and Canadian units, made an amphibious landing behind the German lines near the city of Anzio on 22 January 1944. The Germans quickly surrounded the landing area with strong forces and prevented the Anglo-American forces from marching on to Rome and interdicting the German supply lines to the Monte Cassino front. To assist the US Army units in breaking through the German containment area around Anzio, the 1st Armoured Division (minus CCB) arrived in late January 1944.

Success at Last

Despite repeated attempts, the 1st Armoured Division could not punch its way through the German defensive lines. Rather, it spent most of its time fighting off German counter-attacks on the Anzio beachhead. It took until 23 May 1944, with the German forces around Anzio badly depleted by three months of constant fighting, before the 1st Armoured Division (now reunited with CCB) successfully penetrated the German defensive lines with the support of two infantry divisions. It was then directed to smash through another nearby German defensive line on 29 May 1943.

The employment of the 1st Armoured Division for breaking through successive German defensive lines was against the accepted Armoured Force/Armoured Command doctrine and caused serious losses among its men and equipment. This included 108 medium and 45 light tanks. The task of penetrating enemy defensive lines was supposed to be performed by infantry divisions, with the support of artillery, according to US Army doctrine. Only when the enemy lines were ruptured were armoured divisions to be sent in to exploit the penetration and create havoc in the enemy's rear area, which would include destroying their artillery positions and headquarters units.

An Observation

An officer serving with the 1st Armoured Division in Italy submitted a 'lessons learned' letter to AGF headquarters, which focused on his impressions of the interaction between tanks and infantry units during the break-out from Anzio and subsequent drive into northern Italy. The following extract was included in a memorandum disseminated throughout the US Army for training purposes:

> One more final parting shot, and that is we must get our officers and men to read the book [manual]. They seem to insist upon learning it the hard way. The training books are written as a result of battle experiences and are kept up to date by the hard labors of officers who are continually bringing battle experiences into print. However, the officers and men at the front seem to develop that 'know it all' attitude and that the books are only written for the inexperienced in the rear. Many times, they have explained to me a lesson which they have learned at the expense of a lot of our men when I was able to turn to a page in the book where they could have read and learned without the loss.

The Follow-Up Italian Campaign

A portion of the 1st Armoured Division that broke out from the Anzio beachhead was sent to secure Rome (as part of a task force) and captured the city on 4 June 1944, meeting with little resistance. The seizure of Rome was seen as an important milestone in the Italian campaign. In truth, it did mark a turning-point but not in a positive way as two days later the Allied invasion of Normandy, France, named Operation OVERLORD, took place. Overnight, the Italian campaign became even more of a secondary theatre than it was before, and from that point on received much lower priority in both men and equipment.

Once the break-out from the Anzio beachhead was achieved, the bulk of the 1st Armoured Division was sent northward towards the Arno River in pursuit of retreating German forces. Due to continuing heavy losses in men and equipment, the division was pulled out of the front lines on 22 July 1944 for rest and refitting. During this period, it was reorganized from a 1942 armoured division TO&E into a 1943 armoured division TO&E, as favoured by McNair. The divisional commander, Major General Ernest N. Harmon, passed command of the division to Major General Vernon E. Prichard the same month.

Placed back into the front lines in August 1944, the 1st Armoured Division found itself confronted once again with a new German defensive line. Despite its best efforts and that of the infantry divisions of the American Fifth Army between September and October 1944, the Germans could not be dislodged from their positions. Faced with shortages of both men and equipment and with winter fast approaching, the fighting eventually petered out in October 1944 and did not start up again until March 1945. The 1st Armoured Division was placed into reserve for the winter.

The 1st Armoured Division did not begin to see any significant action again until 14 April 1945, when it was employed in an Anglo-American offensive named Operation GRAPESHOT. This called for the division to advance towards the River

Po, which bisects the 18,000-square mile Po Valley in the uppermost portion of northern Italy.

By 20 April 1945, the 1st Armoured Division penetrated the German defensive lines that had stopped them in October 1944 and entered the Po Valley, crossing the River Po on 23 April 1945. One of its tasks was to prevent retreating German forces from withdrawing into Austria or entering Switzerland. It captured the city of Milan on 30 April 1945. By the time the remaining Axis forces in Italy surrendered on 2 May 1945, the 1st Armoured Division had almost reached the Swiss border with Italy.

There had been hope that secret talks between the American government and the Vichy French senior leadership in North Africa would prevent any fighting during Operation TORCH, which began on 8 November 1942. In anticipation of that, US Army light tanks, such as the preserved M5 example pictured here, had oversized markings applied to avoid being fired upon by Vichy French forces. *(Pierre-Olivier Buan)*

(**Above**) A restored M3A1 Light Tank is seen here, representative of that which would have been used during Operation TORCH. In spite of attempts to convince Vichy French forces North Africa not to oppose Allied landings, the opposite was often the case. It took several days of sometimes fierce fighting before they capitulated and came over to the Allied side. *(Pierre-Olivier Buan)*

(**Opposite, above**) In this wartime picture we see a US Army M3A1 Light Tank coming ashore during Operation TORCH. The 1942 armoured division (heavy) TO&E called for 158 light tanks. Each of the division's two armoured regiments had sixty-three light tanks. In addition, there were seventeen located in the division's armoured reconnaissance company, with fifteen in the division's headquarters company. *(Mike Haines' collection)*

(**Opposite, below**) The amphibious landings of the 1st and 2nd Armoured Divisions in Operation TORCH went reasonably well as they took place generally unopposed. Pictured here are a Half-Track Car M2 and a 0.25-ton 4 × 4 truck (Jeep) of the 1st Armoured Division shortly after coming ashore on 8 November 1942 in French Algeria as part of the Centre Task Force. *(National Archives)*

169

(**Opposite, above**) The Vichy French forces in North Africa had a total of 500 tanks, many of them First World War-era FT Light Tanks. They posed little threat to the M3A1 and M5 Light Tanks of the 1st or 2nd Armoured Divisions and when encountered were easily dealt with. In this picture, we see two abandoned examples of the FT Light Tanks in French North Africa during Operation TORCH. *(National Archives)*

(**Opposite, below**) The 2nd Armoured Division and the separate light tank battalions that took part in Operation TORCH were equipped with the M5 Light Tanks seen here. However, those units did not take part in the fighting for French Tunisia as they could not be supported logistically from French Morocco. The M5 Light Tank had more effective and more reliable power train and running gear compared to that of the M3 and M3A1 Light Tanks, but was hobbled by the same thin armour and obsolete 37mm main gun. *(Patton Museum)*

(**Above**) The 1st Armoured Division was primarily equipped with the M3 Light Tank, with a smaller number of the improved M3A1 Light Tank seen here. On 26 November 1942, the M3 Light Tanks of the 1st Tank Battalion of the 1st Armoured Division were the first American tanks to engage German tanks in battle during the Second World War. They destroyed seven German medium tanks for the loss of six M3 Light Tanks. *(Pierre-Olivier Buan)*

M5
I
USA
W 303748

COIFFEUR
HACHETTE
PHOTOGRAPHIE

(**Opposite, above**) Following the successful conclusion of the campaign to secure French Tunisia from German and Italian forces, the 1st Armoured Division returned to French Morocco to refit and to train replacements. It was at that point the division had its M3 and M3A1 Light Tanks replaced by the M5 Light Tank seen here. This was done despite many stating that it would make more sense to equip the division with only medium tanks. *(Patton Museum)*

(**Opposite, below**) Seen here in a parade in French Morocco, which celebrated the successful conclusion of Operation TORCH, are two T19 Howitzer Motor Carriages (HMC) passing the reviewing stand. Already considered obsolete by this time, they would be found in the three armoured field artillery battalions of both the 1st and 2nd Armoured Divisions during the French North Africa campaign. *(Patton Museum)*

(**Above**) In theory, the 1st and 2nd Armoured Divisions committed to Operation TORCH should have been issued with the M7 Howitzer Motor Carriages (HMC) series as seen here, yet they arrived in theatre with the T19 Howitzer Motor Carriage (HMC). This was due to the fact that the bulk of the early-production units of the M7 had been supplied under Lend-Lease to the British Eighth Army fighting the Afrika Korps in North Africa. *(Pierre-Olivier Buan)*

2△82R

(**Opposite, above**) Under the 1942 armoured division (heavy) TO&E, the 1st and 2nd Armoured Divisions taking part in the French North Africa campaign should have had seventy-nine armoured cars in the inventory, with the majority in the divisions' armoured reconnaissance companies. As the M8 Light Armoured Car did not enter service until March 1943, the requirement was filled by the Scout Car M3A1 seen here or by light tanks. *(Author's collection)*

(**Opposite, below**) Pictured here during a training exercise conducted at the Desert Training Centre in California is an M3 Medium Tank. When the initial elements of the 1st Armoured Division took part in Operation TORCH, its medium tank battalions were still equipped with the M3. When the remaining elements of the division arrived in French Tunisia in January 1943, some of the medium tank battalions had been equipped with the M4 or M4A1 Medium Tanks. *(National Archives)*

(**Above**) The first combat action between the 1st Armoured Division and German forces took place between 28 November and 6 December 1942 at Tebourba, Tunisia. The M3 Medium Tanks of CCB were supporting a British Army infantry operation and blundered into a number of enemy anti-tank traps, suffering serious losses. Pictured is a knocked-out M3 Medium Tank. *(National Archives)*

(**Above**) Unlike the initial medium armoured tank battalions of the 1st Armoured Division that arrived in French North Africa during Operation TORCH with the M3 Medium Tank, the 2nd Armoured Division had completely transitioned to the M4 and M4A1 Medium Tanks before taking part in Operation TORCH. Shown here is an early-production M4A1 Medium Tank with the direct-vision slots in the front hull (glacis). *(Patton Museum)*

(**Opposite, above**) Attached to the 1st Armoured Division during the fighting around Tebourba, Tunisia between 28 November and 6 December 1942 was a platoon of five M4 series Medium Tanks from the 2nd Armoured Division. On the last day of the fighting they were all destroyed by a German tank and anti-tank gun ambush. Pictured here is an M4A1 Medium Tank as a monument tank in France. *(Patton Museum)*

(**Opposite, below**) To deal with the threat posed by German ground-attack aircraft in French North Africa the US Army modified the chassis of the Half-Track Personnel Carrier M3 to create the Combination Gun Motor Carriage (CGMC) T28E1 seen here. It was armed with a 37mm automatic gun and two water-cooled .50 calibre machine guns. It was not organic to armoured divisions but normally attached. *(Patton Museum)*

MUSEE

(**Above**) A progressively-improved version of the Combination Gun Motor Carriage (CGMC) T28E1 employed in French North Africa was the Combination Gun Motor Carriage (CGMC) M15. It in turn led to the final version seen here labelled the M15A1. The M15 and M15A1 both had the T28E1's 37mm automatic gun but changed from water-cooled .50 calibre machine guns to the air-cooled version. *(Paul and Loren Hannah)*

(**Opposite, below**) Along with the development of the combination 37mm automatic gun and .50 calibre machine guns, the Ordnance Department pushed ahead with a modified M3 Half-Track Personnel Carrier armed with a Maxson electrically-powered one-man turret armed with two air-cooled .50 calibre machine guns. That vehicle, seen here, was designated the Multiple Gun Motor Carriage (MGMC) M13. *(Patton Museum)*

(**Opposite, above**) The restored Multiple Gun Motor Carriage (MGMC) M16 shown here was the progressively-improved M13. The same Maxson turret instead mounted four air-cooled .50 calibre machine guns. The vehicle was standardized in December 1942 with production beginning in May 1943 and ending in March 1944 with a total of 3,614 units assembled. Many were upgrades/conversions from previously-manufactured M13s. *(Pierre-Olivier Buan)*

U.S.A.
4083887
RA PD 18534

U.S.A. 406137
D-2
Y5838

V-602TD
D-9

(**Opposite, above**) Somewhere in French Tunisia is this 37mm Gun Motor Carriage (GMC) M6, which was found in both tank destroyer formations as well as in the 1942 armoured division (heavy) TO&E. The vehicle was also designated the WC-55 Truck, 0.75-ton 4 × 4 Gun Motor Carriage (GMC). One Army Ground Force (AGF) observer noted in a report: 'The sending of such a patently inadequate destroyer into combat can best be termed a tragic mistake.' Most were converted to WC-52s by removing the 37mm gun. *(Patton Museum)*

(**Above**) In this picture we see a 75mm Gun Motor Carriage (GMC) M3 in French Tunisia. Two tank destroyer battalions employing the 37mm Gun Motor Carriage M6 and the M3 enjoyed some initial successes against German tanks in November 1942. However, during the February 1943 Battle for Kasserine Pass the same two tank destroyer battalions took heavy losses from German tank units. *(Patton Museum)*

(**Opposite, below**) The eventual replacement for the wheeled tank destroyer M6 and the half-track-based tank destroyer M3 late in the French North Africa campaign was the 3-inch Gun Motor Carriage (GMC) M10. Pictured here is an M10A1. A fair match for German medium tanks in 1943, its main gun lacked the penetrative power to deal with heavily-armoured late-war German tanks and assault guns. *(Pierre-Olivier Buan)*

(**Opposite, above**) The US Army discovered in French North Africa that when German tanks went on the offensive they almost always brought along with them their towed anti-tank guns, such as the dual-purpose 88mm anti-aircraft/anti-tank gun pictured here. These were sited to provide over-watch protection from enemy tank-led counter-attack and proved extremely effective against the US Army in that theatre of conflict. *(Author's collection)*

(**Opposite, below**) During the initial stages of the Battle for Kasserine Pass, two medium tank companies of the 1st Armoured Division, supported by a dozen tank destroyers, counter-attacked the advancing German panzer divisions and charged into a German tank and anti-tank gun ambush and were decimated. Pictured here is a destroyed M4A1 Medium Tank. *(Patton Museum)*

(**Above**) The large number of M4 and M4A1 Medium Tanks lost by the 1st Armoured Division during the Battle for Kasserine Pass had to be quickly made up to maintain the division's battlefield effectiveness. One method involved diverting a battalion's-worth of diesel-engine-powered M4A2 Medium Tanks intended for the British Army, an example of which is seen here, to the 1st Armoured Division. *(Pierre-Olivier Buan)*

Being backed up onto a ship's main deck in preparation for the invasion of the island of Sicily (Operation HUSKY, July one;943) is an M3 Gun Motor Carriage (GMC). By this time, the full-tracked M10 Gun Motor Carriage (GMC) had replaced it in many tank destroyer battalions. Beginning with the invasion of Italy, the M3 was employed as a self-propelled artillery piece. *(National Archives)*

Coming off a landing barge in Sicily during Operation HUSKY is an M4A1 Medium Tank. All the M3 Medium Tanks were out of service by then with the US Army. During this period of the Second World War the M4 and M4A1 Medium Tanks were still held in high regard by the US Army as well the diesel-engine-powered versions used by the British Army, the M4A2 and M4A4. *(Patton Museum)*

On a Sicilian beach is an M2 half-track Scout Car with a large improvised storage container on the rear of its armoured body. In an Armoured Force Board report dated 12 December 1942, it was recommended that the M2 and M3 be replaced by a single half-track vehicle designated the M3A2. This never took place as in March 1944 all new half-track production ended. *(Patton Museum)*

On 19 May 1942, the Ordnance Committee recommended that the interior skate rail that ran around the interior of the Half-Track Scout Car M2 for the attachment of machine guns should be done away with. In its place would be an M32 truck-type ring mount over the right front of the vehicle's passenger compartment as seen here. This modification resulted in the vehicle being designated the Half-Track Scout Car M2A1. *(Patton Museum)*

(**Opposite, above**) Pictured in Italy in November 1943 is an M4A1 Medium Tank. The Western Allies had invaded the country on 3 September 1943. The maximum armour thickness on the front upper hull of both the M4 and M4A1 Medium Tanks was approximately 50mm. Armour thickness on the near-vertical sides of the tanks was about 38mm. *(Patton Museum)*

(**Opposite, below**) At a US Army depot in Italy is an early-production M4 Medium Tank as can be identified by the direct-vision armoured visor cover seen in-between the two soldiers. It also had the early-production narrow cast-armour rotor shield, which formed part of the cast-armour M34 gun shield. The rotor shield was 50mm thick and the gun shield behind it 89mm thick. *(Mike Haines' collection)*

(**Above**) An Ordnance Department wartime display shows all the various things that fit in or on an M4 series Medium Tank. Due to the more angular welded armoured hull of the M4 Medium Tank it had authorized storage for ninety-seven main gun rounds, while the more rounded hull of the cast-armour M4A1 left room for only ninety authorized main gun rounds. *(Patton Museum)*

(**Opposite, above**) Due to the steep slope on the upper front hull of the M4 and M4A1 Medium Tanks, the designers were forced to come up with very narrow overheard hatches for the driver and bow-gunner as is evident from this picture of an M4A1 Medium Tank in Italy. In the hatches for the driver and bow-gunner were 360-degree rotating and tilting periscopes. *(Patton Museum)*

(**Above**) A column of US Army M4A1 Medium Tanks drive through a badly-damaged Italian city. They can be identified as early-production units by their single overhead turret hatch for the vehicle commander. The Medium Tanks M4 and M4A1 did not start leaving the factory floor with overhead loader turret hatches until November 1943. *(Mike Haines' collection)*

(**Opposite, below**) In this picture taken at a US Army depot in Italy we see both the welded-armour-hull M4 Medium Tanks and the cast-armour-hull M4A1 tanks. The M4 Medium Tank in the centre of the front row has the full-width M34A1 rotor shield, while all the others pictured have the early-production M34 narrow rotor gun shield. *(Mike Haines' collection)*

(**Above**) The M4A1 Medium Tank pictured here has the early-production three-piece differential and final drives arrangement from the prototype T6 Medium Tank. It consisted of a large three-piece cast-armour housing that bolted together to form the lower front of the vehicle's hull. Eventually, a one-piece cast-armour housing was produced for the entire M4 series of medium tanks. *(Patton Museum)*

(**Opposite, above**) The M8 Howitzer Motor Carriage (HMC) seen here was considered an assault gun somewhat akin to the German turretless assault guns. Unlike its German counterparts capable only of direct fire, the M8 could be employed in both the direct and indirect fire modes. For anti-tank purposes the 75mm howitzer on the M8 was provided with a shaped-charge round, designated the High-Explosive Anti-Tank (HEAT) M66 shell. *(Pierre-Olivier Buan)*

(**Opposite, below**) In a February 1944 US Army manual appears this description of the M8 Light Armoured Car and its role: 'Armored cars are the basic command and communication vehicle ... capable of cruising 100 to 200 miles cross-country or 200 to 400 miles on highways without refueling. On a level, improved road, it can sustain a speed of 55mph.' Each M8 had both a long-range and a short-range radio set. *(Pierre-Olivier Buan)*

405958
EDITH

USA
7
3A-42C
B-18

817

U.S.A.
DEAD EYE DICK

(**Opposite, above**) Somewhere in Italy a US Army 0.25-ton 4 × 4 truck (Jeep) passes by a destroyed German Army Panzer IV medium tank. Each of the two armoured regiments in the 1942 armoured division (light) had an authorized strength of eighty-four Jeeps. The single armoured infantry regiment of the 1942 armoured division (light) was authorized fifty-seven Jeeps. *(National Archives)*

(**Above**) An M5 Light Tank crosses a portable bridge in Italy. An April 1944 US Army report from the Italian theatre stated that like the M4 Medium Tank series, the M5 Light Tank was mechanically satisfactory, but its armament was no longer adequate. It was also felt that both the M4 Medium Tank and M5 Light Tank needed lightweight steel track with chevron-type treads for better off-road mobility. *(Patton Museum)*

(**Opposite, below**) By the time the fighting ended in Italy in May 1945, total losses in US Army M5 Light Tanks, an example of which is pictured here, amounted to 424 units. With the M4 and M4A1 Medium Tanks, total losses were listed at 1,072 units. There were 111 of the M8 Light Armoured Cars destroyed and 72 units of its variant, the M20 Armoured Utility Car. *(National Archives)*

(**Above**) In this close-up picture of an M4A1 Medium Tank in Italy we can see on the left side of the turret the so-called 'pistol port', which was in fact a misnomer. In practice, the port was employed as a means to load main gun ammunition into the vehicle. Seen as a ballistic weak spot, it was deleted on the production lines beginning in April 1943, only to be reinstated in November 1943. *(Patton Museum)*

(**Opposite, above**) Taken in the Italian theatre is this picture of an M7 series Howitzer Motor Carriage (HMC) with its weapon in full recoil. The armoured field artillery battalions of both the 1942/43 armoured divisions were sub-divided into three batteries of six M7 series HMCs each. The armoured field artillery battalions were overseen by a headquarters and service company. *(National Archives)*

(**Opposite, below**) The gun crew of an M7 series Howitzer Motor Carriage (HMC) prepare for their next fire mission. Each of the six-gun batteries of the armoured field artillery battalions of the armoured divisions also included seven M3 Half-Track Personnel Carriers. These were employed in a number of roles including as ammunition carriers and as platforms for the battery commander and the maintenance section. *(Patton Museum)*

(**Above**) Pictured here are two of the M32 tank recovery vehicles in Italy. The 1943 armoured division (light) had twenty-four units as part of its TO&E. There were five in each of the division's three tank battalions and two in each of the division's three armoured field artillery battalions. Each of the division's three armoured infantry battalions had one M32 assigned. *(Mike Haines' collection)*

(**Opposite, above**) A crucial element for the successful functioning of an armoured division, be it the 1942 or 1943 TO&E, was radio communications. This task was overseen by the signal company. Teams from the signal company were attached to the CC headquarters units as well as the division's rear echelon. The division's high-powered radios as seen here were found in the division's headquarters forward echelon. *(National Archives)*

(**Opposite, below**) The armoured engineer battalions of both the 1942 and 1943 TO&E performed a wide variety of tasks, including the location of mines/minefields and their clearance. Pictured here is an engineer with a SCR-625 mine detector. The armoured engineer battalion was broken down into a headquarters company, three engineer companies and a medical detachment. *(National Archives)*

HQ40

(**Above**) Within the armoured engineer battalion in the 1943 armoured division TO&E each company had a bulldozer as seen here. These were employed in numerous roles including removing battlefield obstacles, natural or man-made. Elements of the engineer companies, or entire companies, were typically in the leading elements of an armoured division's CCs as they advanced. *(Pierre-Olivier Buan)*

(**Opposite, above**) An M1 Heavy Wrecker of an armoured division ordnance maintenance battalion is shown switching out the air-cooled radial engine of an M4A1 Medium Tank. In the armoured division, the senior ordnance officer was in charge of the acquisition and distribution of everything from ammunition to automotive spare parts. He was also in charge of the salvage, maintenance and repair of all ordnance equipment. *(Patton Museum)*

(**Opposite, below**) The medical detachment for each tank battalion of both the 1942 and 1943 armoured division TO&Es included three of the Half-Track Personnel Carrier M3 configured as armoured ambulances. In addition, each tank battalion medical detachment included five 0.25-ton 4 × 4 trucks (Jeeps) and three other larger wheeled ambulances. *(Patton Museum)*

U S A
HURRICANE

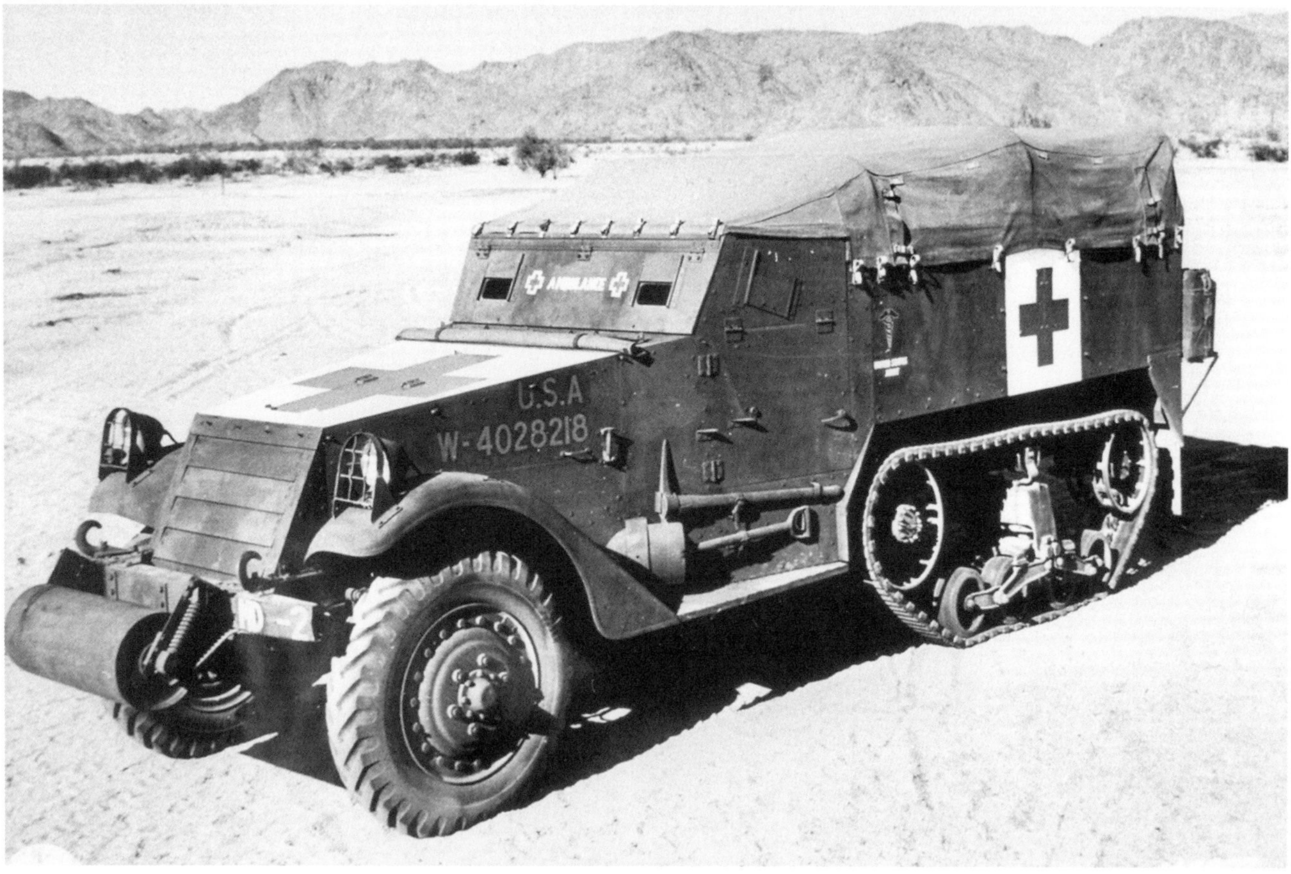
AMBULANCE
U.S.A
W-4028218

(**Above**) Reflecting the fact that tanks were typically at the forefront of fighting and often difficult for ambulances and medical personnel to reach, the tank crews were taught to perform a basic level of first-aid from the medical kits provided on the tanks and evacuate their wounded comrades on their own as is seen here. *(Patton Museum)*

(**Opposite, above**) Before tank battalions entered into combat their medical detachments would assemble an aid station at the battalion's assembly area. Every time the tank battalion advanced a certain distance, the aid station would be disassembled and re-established at the next assembly point. An important element of transporting the wounded from the battlefield to the aid stations were the litter-bearers, seen here in action. *(National Archives)*

(**Opposite, below**) In this picture we see a second-generation M4A3 Medium Tank armed with a 76mm main gun and designated the M4A3(76)W by the Ordnance Department. The first examples arrived in Italy for the 1st Armoured Division in the late summer of 1944. It dispensed with the armoured gun rotor seen on first-generation models and instead had the full-width gun shield shown here. *(Pierre-Olivier Buan)*

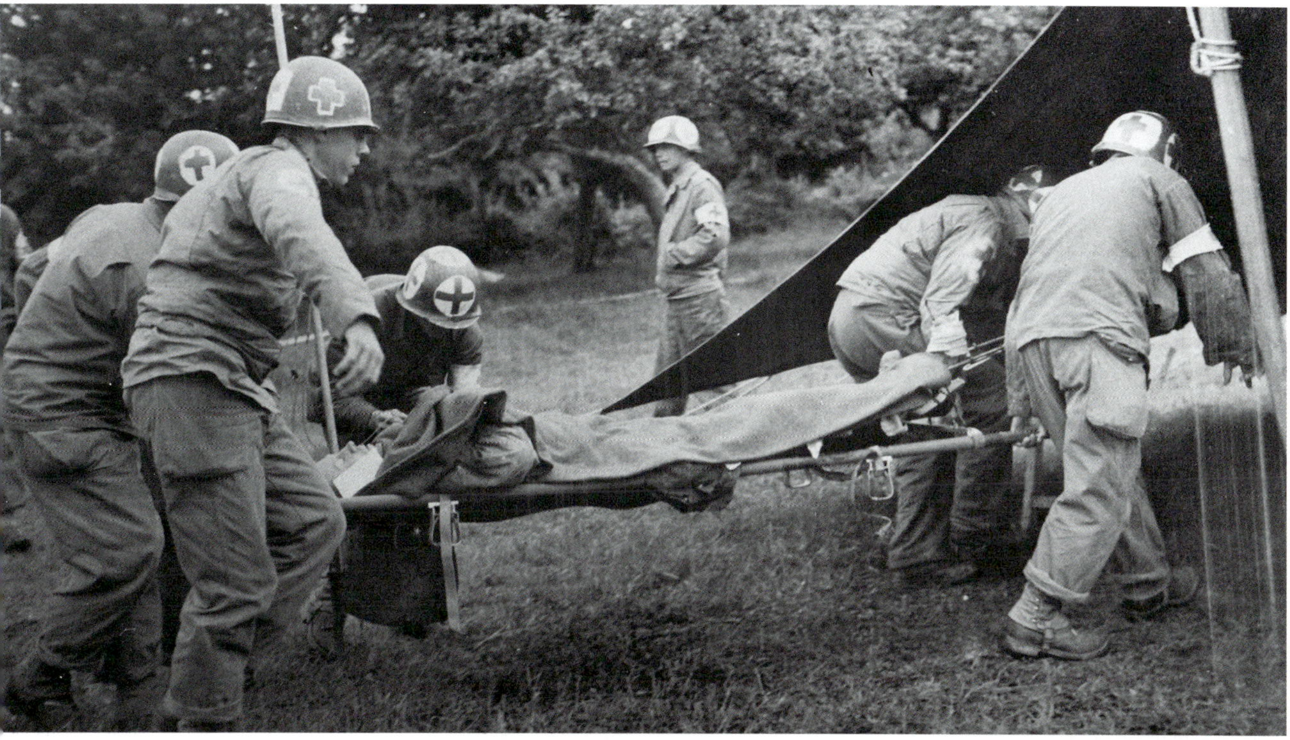

(**Above**) In a US Army depot in Italy we see a second-generation M4A3(76)W Medium Tank with the original vertical volute spring suspension (VVSS) system. Behind it is a first-generation M4A1 Medium Tank with a 75mm main gun. The upper front hull plate on the second-generation M4 series Medium Tanks were set at a less steep angle than that of the first-generation models. *(Mike Haines' collection)*

(**Opposite, above**) A small number of pilot (pre-production) units of what later became the 76mm Gun Motor Carriage (GMC) M18 were tested at Anzio but proved unpopular due to being too cramped for their crews and too thinly-armoured. Only one tank destroyer battalion employed the M18 as pictured in Italy, beginning in late 1944. The preferred tank destroyer in theatre was the 3-inch Gun Motor Carriage (GMC) M10. *(Author's collection)*

(**Opposite, below**) Found in US Army armoured divisions was the 12-ton 6 x 4 Truck M20 seen here. A twelve-wheel Trailer M9 was normally towed behind the M20 truck. The truck had a loaded weight of 45,000lb, with the trailer having a payload capacity of approximately 90,000lb. It was employed to recover vehicles along improved roads and was not capable of recovering vehicles off-road. *(Christophe Vallier)*

20
1A
TD

U.S.A. 4822191
WSU 625

(**Opposite, above**) Pictured here is a 4-ton 6 × 6 cargo truck that was identified by the builder as the Diamond T968. It had a cargo capacity of 8,000lb and was capable of towing a 12,000lb trailer. The vehicle came in different body styles, including wrecker and dump truck. As supplied to the corps of engineers it was fitted with a number of different specialized bodies including carrying and launching treadway bridge sections. Only early-production examples came with an enclosed cab. *(Christophe Vallier)*

(**Opposite, below**) Showing up in the European Theatre of Operations (ETO) in December 1944 in small numbers was the M24 Light Tank pictured here. It appeared in the Italian theatre in the spring of 1945. In armoured divisions it was tasked with secondary duties, such as escorting armoured infantry units or in the reconnaissance or flank security roles. *(Author's collection)*

(**Above**) A dependable and reliable vehicle, the M24 Light Tank differed from its predecessors in that it had an Ordnance Department-developed torsion-bar suspension, which provided greatly-improved off-road mobility. It could go, reports stated, where the M5 and M4 simply couldn't go. Earlier light tanks had ridden on a version of the vertical volute spring suspension (VVSS) system like those on the first generation of M4 Medium Tanks. *(Author's collection)*

Chapter Four

Battlefield Maturity

The first US Army armoured division to arrive in the United Kingdom was the 3rd Armoured Division in September 1943, followed by the 2nd Armoured Division, shipped in from Sicily in November 1943. Both divisions retained the 1942 armoured division TO&E until the conclusion of the war in Europe.

Three more armoured divisions arrived in the United Kingdom in 1944 from the United States, prior to Operation OVERLORD, the Allied invasion of France on 6 June 1944. These were the 4th, 5th and 6th Armoured Divisions. All of them were based on the 1943 armoured division TO&E, as were all the subsequent armoured divisions shipped overseas. No US Army armoured divisions would see service in the Pacific Theatre of Operation during the Second World War.

The 7th through to the 12th Armoured Divisions arrived in the United Kingdom from the United States, following Operation OVERLORD, between 13 June 1944 and October 1944. The 14th Armoured Division was shipped from the United States directly to France in October 1944, as was the 13th Armoured Division, which arrived in France in January 1945.

The 16th and 20th Armoured Divisions both arrived in France from the United States in February 1945 and were assigned to the 15th Army Group until such time that they were required for front-line service by an army. Both were eventually transferred to the control of Patton's Third Army in April 1945.

The Battle of the Hedgerows

Elements of the 2nd Armoured Division initially landed in France on 9 June 1944 and were committed to combat on 13 June 1944. The remainder of the division arrived by the end of June and all were placed into action on 2 July 1944. The initial elements of the 3rd Armoured Division arrived in France on 24 June 1944 and entered into combat on 29 June 1944. The remainder of the division arrived on 9 July 1944. Both divisions formed part of the First Army, under General Omar Bradley.

The area of France that the First Army had seized was poorly-suited to the employment of armoured divisions. The biggest natural obstacle was the hedgerows, which divided the region into small plots of land. This led to a series of small-scale engagements by the 2nd and 3rd Armoured Divisions in support of the First Army's infantry divisions, which was against the accepted Armoured Command (formerly the Armoured Force) doctrine. However, a constant shortage of infantrymen forced Bradley to push them into the front lines.

During the subsequent fighting, labelled as 'The Battle of the Hedgerows' by US Army historians, which took place between 6 June and 24 July 1944, the US Army's lack of emphasis on training between the infantry and tankers (be it separate battalions or armoured divisions) prior to their arrival overseas, caused serious losses and resulting problems between them. This is illustrated in a passage from a US Army History Centre publication by Michael D. Doubler titled *Busting the Bocage: American Combined Arms Operations in France, June 6–31 July 1944*:

> Tank-infantry coordination was particularly poor and resulted in violent outbursts between tankers and infantrymen. At least one infantry commander threatened to shoot an armour officer for failing to support an attack, and one tank commander threatened to gun down infantrymen who provided inadequate local security for his vehicle.

The importance of pre-battle training between infantry and tanks was realized long before the invasion of Normandy, France, but was not sufficiently emphasized. This training memo sent out by the Second Army headquarters on 5 May 1942 illustrates that point:

> To insure maximum support, it is essential that tank and supported troops be trained as a combat team. In training with tanks, foot troops should be given practice in advancing by fire and movement behind, and in cooperation with tanks, in passing through barbed wire crushed by tanks and mopping up behind them. During combined training, troops must become familiar with flag signals and combat methods of small tank units.

A major problem was the fact that the smaller AM infantry radios, such as the handheld SCR-536 'handie-talkie', could not talk to the FM radios of the tanks or any other vehicle in the armoured division. This made combined-arms training very difficult. FM radios had been introduced into the armoured divisions in 1941 as the original AM radios on the tanks and other vehicles were subject to both static and various other forms of interference, making them extremely unreliable when moving. German tanks and other armoured fighting vehicles employed AM radios before and during the Second World War.

There were a number of improvisations made by both the infantrymen and tankers to deal with the hedgerows. The best-known to this day was by Sergeant Curtis G. Culin of the 2nd Armoured Division. He proposed that the division's tanks be fitted on their lower front hull with sharp steel prongs made from the leftover German beach obstacles. So equipped, the tanks could push through hedgerows rather than trying to climb over them, exposing their thinly-armoured hull bottoms to enemy fire. These improvised devices went by a number of different nicknames including 'Culin cutters' or 'hedgerow prongs'. Because the Culin cutter when fitted to both light and medium tanks resembled tusks, vehicles so fitted were sometimes known as 'rhino tanks'.

In conjunction with the creation of rhino tanks, both the 2nd and 3rd Armoured Divisions began conducting behind-the-lines infantry and tank training exercises. This pre-battle training combined with new methods of tank-infantry radio communications greatly aided in turning the tide of battle within the hedgerows in the US Army's favour.

Break-Out and Pursuit

Bradley could now consider that he had the means at his disposal to break through the bocage. He put into action an offensive operation code-named Operation COBRA, which ran from 25 to 28 July 1944. It involved eight infantry divisions and two armoured divisions, the 2nd and 3rd. The latter were tasked for employment during the exploitation phase of the fighting when the infantry divisions had broken through the enemy defensive lines. This was established Armoured Command doctrine.

By 27 July 1944, Operation COBRA was considered a success as German organized resistance began to crumble. On 31 July 1944, the last of the German defensive forces opposing the First Army ceased to exist. From a passage in a post-war US Army report by Lieutenant Colonel Briard P. Johnson titled 'The Operations of the Second Armored Division in the Saint Lo Breakout, July 26–30 July 1944' is an account of the losses it inflicted on the opposing German forces during Operation COBRA:

> In a three-day period of action, 2nd Armored Division had advanced against heavy resistance over 20 miles behind the main German forces to the north, successfully blocked efforts of major German forces to escape to the south, and had assumed a major role in the destruction of German forces ... 323 captured, an estimated 1,500 killed, and about 300 vehicles of all types including 74 half-tracks, 20 tanks reported by type, plus many other tanks and tank-like self-propelled guns included in a hurried partial count. In addition, hundreds if not thousands of vehicles and thousands more prisoners taken or destroyed by day air action against the German columns whose withdrawal was blocked by the armored action [of the 2nd Armoured Division].

For the Germans, the situation had become a *Riesensauerei* ('giant pigpen'). The commander of the German Seventh Army, that had fought so hard to keep the First Army contained in its lodgement area, telephoned Hitler's headquarters on 31 July to say '... if the Americans get through Avranches [a city in France] they will be out of the woods and they'll be able to do whatever they want.' A US Army infantry division seized the now-destroyed city on 20 August 1944.

Patton's Third Army

On 1 August 1944 Bradley ordered Patton's Third Army into action as the Operation COBRA breakthrough turned into a break-out. Patton put the 4th, 5th and 6th Armoured Divisions at the head of the Third Army and set them loose in a classic exploitation on the badly-organized German forces in their paths. The 4th had arrived in France on 13 July, the 5th on 25 July and the 6th on 18 July 1944.

In a 2011 interview by US Army armour branch historian Robert S. Cameron with Brigadier General (retired) Albin F. Irzyk, who eventually rose to command the 8th Tank Battalion of the 4th Armoured Division, the latter described the typical offensive formation his battalion employed in their drive across the ETO:

> When we moved out, I would usually have a couple of platoons of light tanks, a tank company, and some recon. That is the way we went into combat, but we adjusted. Later, when I took the battalion, I fought the battalion as I thought it should have been done. There's no set way. Every commander organizes the battalion as he thinks it should be, and it has to change, depending on what the situation is. If we're moving rapidly, we get the lighter forces out in front. If we're held up, we put the medium tanks up. So, we have to make adjustments by the minute.

The 4th Armoured Division would remain part of Patton's Third Army throughout the Second World War, with the 6th Armoured Division spending the bulk of the war as part of the Third Army. The 7th Armoured Division set foot in France on 10 August 1944 and entered into combat three days later as part of the Third Army. It remained part of the Third Army until 25 September 1944 when it was transferred to the First Army. The 5th Armoured Division served as part of the Third Army from 1 to 26 August 1944, when it was then transferred to the First Army.

From Patton's 'Letters of Instruction No. 3' appear his thoughts on the employment of armoured divisions based on his experiences in French North Africa, Sicily and in the ETO:

> In an armored division, as in an infantry division, attacks must be coordinated; and the infantry, and the tanks, and the guns [artillery] must work as a unit. Whenever possible, it is desirable that the guns operate under divisional control and with their forward observers in tanks, immediately take under fire enemy antitank guns, and either reduce them or blind them with smoke or white phosphorus. Success depends upon the coordinated use of the guns and the

tanks, with the guns paying particular attention to hostile artillery, and above all too antitank guns and [enemy] observation posts.

Armoured Divisional Commanders

During the first twelve days of August 1944, the fast-charging and aggressive 4th Armoured Division captured almost 5,000 German prisoners and destroyed or captured 250 enemy vehicles. The division was commanded by Major General John S. Woods, nicknamed 'Tiger Jack'. Before his division shipped out to the ETO, Woods informed his men: 'This division will attack and attack, and if an order is given to fall back, that order will not have come from me.'

Liddell Hart, the famous British military historian, described Woods of the 4th Armoured Division as 'The Rommel of American Armoured Forces … one of the most dynamic commanders of armour in World War II and the first in the Allied Armies to demonstrate the essence of the art and tempo of handling a mobile force.' US Army Lieutenant General Willis D. Crittenberger (corps commander in the Italian theatre) said of Wood, 'He far exceeded in his leadership capabilities any man I have ever known.'

The 6th Armoured Division was commanded by Major General W. Grow. Patton would describe Grow as 'one of the best Armored Forces commanders the war produced.' Under Grow's command, the 6th Armoured Division penetrated some 200 miles into enemy territory in Brittany, France; the longest independent operation by a single division (armour or infantry) of the US Army during the Second World War. Grow would remark after the war that his division 'had performed the greatest cavalry-type operation of the war … [and] had proved the soundness of the … mechanized division and the hard months of training.'

Keep Going

Upon securing the Brittany peninsula in Normandy, Patton sent the 4th and 7th Armoured Divisions eastward towards the River Seine, the last major natural obstacle before Paris. The First Army was also pushing its armoured divisions towards the Seine. On the morning of 23 August 1944, the 7th Armoured Division of Patton's Third Army managed to cross the river despite heavy resistance.

In August 1944, the First Army had under its control the 2nd, 3rd and 5th Armoured Divisions. Besides the 4th and 7th Armoured Divisions, the Third Army still had the 6th Armoured Division. Adequate fuel supplies for both the First Army and Patton's Third Army were becoming an issue in August 1944. Patton urged on his armoured divisions ever deeper into France and even Germany, if possible, before the fuel supply situation became even more critical and would bring all operations to a halt.

From the historical files of the 5th Armoured Division Association comes this brief description by Lieutenant Marvin W. Orgill, commander of a platoon of five medium tanks advancing through France on the way to Germany:

> You begin to get that tingling feeling in the back of your neck. There's no good reason for it, but you get it, and whenever you feel it, you usually run into trouble. You tell your gunner to spatter the patch of woods ahead and he does it with his machine gun. Other tanks join in. Then from the woods come a spurt of flame. If you're lucky the shell misses. You talk your gunner into the target, and in five seconds he fires the 75mm. He fires again and his second shot is on target. Three more rounds go out fast. Your platoon has deployed to the right and left and all are firing now. Suddenly, there is an explosion in the woods, and a German vehicle ahead begins to burn. Two more explosions and two more fires, your stomach begins to uncurl.

September Activities

Between 11 and 17 September 1944, the 4th Armoured Division encircled the French city of Nancy. Well aware that the capture of small or large urban centres was not suited to an armoured division (it was not even addressed in Armoured Command manuals), every division developed its own method to handle such occasions. The 4th Armoured Division left the actual capture of Nancy to an infantry division.

When confronted with small enemy-occupied villages and towns the 4th Armoured Division often dealt with them by simply overrunning them before the Germans knew they were near. When the enemy was alerted and prepared to defend a village or town, the 4th Armoured Division relied on other methods to subdue them as seen in this memo of 23 September 1944: 'There is no further occasion to spare towns in our advances towards Germany. They should be plastered by artillery or air bombardment prior to the entry of our troops.'

German Armour Counter-Attacks

In response to the capture of Nancy and in an effort to cut off Patton's Third Army drive towards the River Rhine and Germany, Hitler ordered a series of counter-attacks in the direction of the 4th Armoured Division between 18 and 25 September 1944. The division was then located near the small French farming town of Arracourt.

Upon the commencement of the German counter-attacks, the 4th Armoured Division, with an attached self-propelled tank destroyer battalion, quickly moved from an offensive role to the defensive role. Aiding them was a single CC from the 6th Armoured Division. Masterfully led by Wood and his able battalion commanders, the division threw back all the German tank-led attacks. This was a very different outcome from what had happened at the Battle for Kasserine Pass in February 1943 and showed how far some US Army armoured divisions had come in their combat effectiveness.

In the ensuing engagements fought around Arracourt, the 4th Armoured Division destroyed eighty-six German tanks and self-propelled guns, while losing forty-eight of their own. From a US Army History Branch publication titled *The 4th Armored Division in the Encirclement of Nancy* by Dr Christopher R. Gabel is this extract describing what made the division the premier exponent of mobile warfare in the ETO:

> Synchronization was also a hallmark of the 4th Armored Division operations. Intensive emphasis on combined arms during training led to the closest of coordination in battle among the arms and services at the company and battalion level. This highly effective teamwork extended to the division's close relationship with the XIX Tactical Air Command. Timely, violent execution by all elements was a byword to the 4th Armored Division philosophy, as was the exploitation of the shock that such synchronization creates.

Armoured Division Doctrinal Issues

Major General Ernest N. Harmon, commander of the 1st Armoured Division beginning in April 1943, would comment on a particular point that he observed in the Mediterranean theatre of operations that he disliked:

> Throughout the African and Italian campaigns there was a continued demand to split the armored division and attach part of its troops to another force. The armored division, like any other division, has been developed as a team, and the full success of its power can only be reaped when it acts as a unit and has all of its strength available for use.

Harmon was only repeating what was in the *Armored Force Field Manual: Tactics and Technique* that was first released in March 1942, which stated: 'The most decisive results will be gained from the grouping of overpowering masses of armored units and launching them against vital objectives deep in the hostile rear. The armored mass must be supported by sufficient means to maintain its momentum until the objective has been attained.'

In the 1944 version of the *Armored Command Field Manual: The Armored Division* there was a refinement of the armoured division main role in the US Army: 'The armored division is organized primarily to perform missions that require great mobility and firepower. It is capable of engaging in most forms of combat but its primary role is an offensive operation against hostile rear areas.' Patton would write: 'The primary mission of armored units is the attacking of infantry and artillery. The enemy's rear area is the happy hunting ground for armor; use every means to get it there.'

There was a serious negative aspect to the Armoured Force/Armoured Command doctrine on the tank's primary objective being the enemy's rear areas and not enemy tank formations as it was with other armies. This meant that its medium tanks had been designed for dealing with soft targets, while specialized tank-destroyers dealt with enemy tanks when encountered. By default, this left US Army medium tanks ill-suited to deal with late-war German medium and heavy tanks when encountered. This is seen in a passage from a March 1945 report from the 2nd Armoured Division by Corporal James A. Miller, a medium tank gunner. In it he describes his frustrations with the apparent lack of muzzle velocity on his 75mm main gun:

> I have been in combat several times in a tank and I found it is silly to try to fight the German tank. One morning in Puffendorf, Germany, about daylight I saw German tanks coming across the field towards us; we all opened fire on them but we had just about as well as have fired our shots straight up into the air for all the good we could do. Every round would bounce off and wouldn't do a bit of damage. I fired at one 800 yards away; he had his side toward me. I hit him from the turret to the bottom and from the front of the tank to the back directly in the side but he never halted ... In my opinion, if we had a gun with plenty of muzzle velocity we would have wiped them out. We out-gunned them but our guns were worthless.

The US Army armoured divisions were generally able to overcome the wide disparity in the battlefield capabilities between its tanks and those of the Germans in the ETO for a number of different reasons. One of these was that US Army armoured divisions seldom encountered large numbers of German tanks. Engagements between American tanks and their enemy counterparts tended to be small-unit actions with no more than a dozen tanks in total being involved on both sides.

For the majority of the fighting in Western Europe, Allied air superiority and fighting in combined-arms formations such as the 4th Armoured Division had at Arracourt offset the firepower and armour protection advantages enjoyed by individual or small numbers of late-war German tanks. Another factor that aided the US Army armoured divisions in the closing stages of the war was the declining skill-sets of German tankers and their leadership. Colonel William Hamburg of the 5th Armoured Division noticed in the last year of the war in the ETO that 'in many cases, the German tank crews were missing shots they shouldn't have.'

New Operations

With the supply of fuel and other equipment becoming ever more tenuous by the end of September 1944, the 4th Armoured Division's fast-moving advance across France since the beginning of Operation COBRA on 1 August 1944 had taken a toll on both men and equipment. Its tanks had averaged 1,000 miles and the division's supply trucks almost 3,000 miles. The division was therefore put into reserve as of 12 October 1944 for a month of rest and refitting.

The 4th Armoured Division returned to the front lines in early November 1944 in anticipation of a new Third Army offensive operation aimed at the River Rhine and Germany. For that planned Third Army offensive, Patton also had the 6th and 10th Armoured Divisions, the 10th having become part of the Third Army on 23 October 1944. It would remain with the Third Army until 1 April 1945 when it became part of the Seventh Army.

The Lorraine Campaign

The Third Army's operations in France from 1 September to 16 December 1944 are referred to by US Army historians as the Lorraine campaign. By its conclusion, the Third Army had lost 403 tanks and suffered 55,182 casualties, with little success due to the terrain, weather and strong German resistance and defensive positions.

Wood was replaced as commander of the 4th Armoured Division on 3 December 1944 by Major General Hugh J. Gaffey, supposedly for health reasons. Many think that his relief was due to serious conflicts between Wood and his corps commander over the mishandling of his division. Wood would comment after the war on the misuse of his division during the Lorraine campaign:

> Aggressive warfare requires constant pressure on the enemy. Commanders must at times demand operations under the most unfavorable circumstances of terrain and weather, and with little regard to the characteristics of the forces at hand. This is unfortunate but it is war. Such were the operations of the 4th Armored Division in the Sarre-Moselle area in the winter of 1944. They show what courage and determination can accomplish in an extremely difficult situation. Beyond that, they furnish only a classical example of the manner in which armored divisions should never be employed, if avoidable. It is hoped that better balancing of forces and better conceptions of battle will prevent any such use of armor in the future.

Armoured Infantry Problems

The issue of armoured divisions having sufficient armoured infantry for their various missions was a continuing challenge from the 1940 TO&E up till the 1943 TO&E. Casualties among armoured infantry units in the ETO through to the end of the war were extremely high due to close working relationships with the tanks in the front lines. From a November 1944 manual titled *The Armored Infantry Battalion* appears this passage on their battlefield tactics and disadvantages:

> Armored infantry normally fights dismounted. Under favorable conditions vehicular armament either mounted or dismounted is used to support the

attack. If vehicles are used, they must be placed in position defilade and dispersed. It moves forward in vehicles until it is forced by enemy fire, or unfavorable terrain, to dismount. In mounted movement, it is sensitive to mine fields, other obstacles, unfavorable terrain, and weather.

The divisional commanders of both the 1942 and 1943 armoured divisions strongly felt that at least three additional armoured infantry battalions should become organic to their respective TO&Es. Some armoured divisions made up for their shortfalls of armoured infantrymen by turning their mortarmen and towed anti-tank gun crewmen into armoured infantrymen.

Certain armoured divisional commanders had their armoured infantrymen ride the tanks into battle. This practice was mentioned in an armoured infantry manual dated November 1944, wherein it was stated that there were three situations that lent themselves to armoured infantrymen riding atop tanks:

1. When it is desired to avoid traffic congestion by withholding the organic vehicles of the infantry temporarily. These vehicles will follow as soon as the traffic conditions of the roads permit.
2. When the terrain is unsuitable for the organic vehicles of the armored infantry.
3. When close mutual support is desired and maximum coordination must be achieved.

The 5th Armoured Division endorsed this practice as seen in this extract from a book titled *Mobility, Shock and Firepower: The Emergence of the US Army's Armor Branch, 1917–1945* by Robert S. Cameron:

> In June 1944, while still in England, the division commander reorganized his division. He matched an equivalent number of tank and infantry companies within each combat command. He further 'married' tanks and infantry squads. Because the armored infantry platoon possessed five squads and each tank platoon included five tanks, each squad was assigned to a single tank. The division employed this reconfiguration through the end of the war. Formation personnel believed this structure maximized tactical cohesion and minimized casualties. From its entrance into combat on 2 August until the end of April 1945, the division's losses totaled 3,043 casualties and 116 tanks. The 6th and 7th Armored Divisions also entered combat within days of the 5th Armored Division yet suffered greater personnel and matériel losses during the same period.

In the ETO it was not uncommon practice for armoured divisions to borrow infantry battalions or even regiments from adjoining infantry divisions to complete their missions whenever it was possible. As these standard line infantry units lacked the training provided to their armoured infantry counterparts they often had difficulty in matching the operational tempo of the tank battalions to which they were attached. In addition, the armoured division that borrowed these line infantry units had to provide them with trucks so they could keep up with the tanks.

Other Armoured Divisions

As part of the First Army, its three armoured divisions – the 2nd, 3rd and 5th – crossed into Belgium in early September 1944. The 7th Armoured Division of the Third Army had entered into combat in France on 13 August 1944. It advanced into The Netherlands in early September 1944. The division was transferred to the First Army on 25 September 1944 and then to the Ninth Army on 8 October 1944. Not being particularly well led by its original division commander, he was replaced on 1 November 1944.

The tanks of the First Army's armoured divisions were worn out after the mad dash across France in August 1944. Despite having a theoretical strength of 1,010 medium tanks between its armoured divisions and separate tank battalions, only 85 per cent were on hand in September 1944. Those tanks present were badly in need of maintenance. The 3rd Armoured Division reported on 18 September 1944 that of an authorized strength of 232 medium tanks, only 70 to 75 were in suitable condition for front-line service.

On 11 September 1944, a platoon from the cavalry reconnaissance squadron from the 5th Armoured Division was the first to cross into Germany. As the remainder of the 5th Armoured Division and the other First and Ninth Army armoured divisions entered Germany they became part of what US Army historians refer to as the Siegfried Line campaign. It began on 11 September 1944 and concluded on 16 December 1944. As part of that campaign the 2nd Armoured Division encircled and cut off the German city of Aachen between 2 and 21 October 1944. The actual capture of the city was left to an infantry division, as had happened with the French city of Nancy the month before.

Major General Ernest N. Harmon had become the 2nd Armoured Division commander on 12 September 1944, replacing Major General Edward H. Brook. The 3rd Armoured Division was the first through the Siegfried Line. It was commanded by Major General Maurice Rose, who was killed on 30 March 1945. He was the highest-ranking US Army officer killed in the ETO by enemy fire. The 5th Armoured Division was commanded by Major General Lunsford E. Oliver.

For the armoured divisions involved in the Siegfried Line campaign it was a frustrating period with little chance for exploitation operations as they, like the armoured divisions of Patton's Third Army, were confined by terrain, weather and strong German resistance supported by well-built defensive positions.

The Battle of the Bulge

The most powerful German counter-offensive operation on the Western Front was launched at the American First Army in the early morning of 16 December 1944. Best known as the 'Battle of the Bulge', it involved almost a million men and consisted of numerous battles over a fairly wide area of Belgium and Germany.

Twelve US Army armoured divisions in the ETO eventually took part in bringing the German counter-offensive to a halt and then pushing it back to its original starting-point. One of the most crucial US Army armoured division engagements early in the Battle of the Bulge occurred at the small Belgian crossroad town of St. Vith. CCB of the 7th Armoured Division rushed in from 26 miles away before the Germans arrived and successfully defended it for five days before withdrawing in good order. The 7th Armoured Division was commanded at the time by Major General Robert W. Hasbrouck.

The brief stand of the 7th Armoured Division's CCB at St. Vith managed to throw off the German planned schedule for the operation and hastened its failure. In conjunction with other units, the 7th Armoured Division delayed the advance of *Kampfgruppe* Peiper, the main armoured spearhead or *Schwerpunkt* of the offensive. Again, this was very different from what had occurred at the Battle for Kasserine Pass in February 1943. From a US Army Centre for Military History publication titled *A Historical Example of Armor in the Defense: The Battle of St. Vith, Belgium, 17–23 December 1944* appears this passage from the 'lessons learned' section:

> Armor is generally thought of as an offensive force. However, its capabilities in defense are great. It conducts an aggressive and an elastic defense. It 'rolls with the punches.' It seeks opportunities to strike when the enemy leaves an opening. It trades terrain for time and tactical advantage, and in so doing makes the enemy pay heavily for the gains which he makes. Finally, it disengages and strikes again from a new direction.

Both the 2nd and 3rd Armoured Divisions of the First Army would also play an important role during the Battle of the Bulge. The latter was in reserve for rest and refitting when the German attack began. In response, the CCs of the division were parcelled out to assist various infantry divisions in the ensuing panic. This was against accepted Armoured Command doctrine and was not resolved until 25 December 1944 when all the division's CCs were brought back together. The division was at that point also reinforced with several infantry units and tied in with the defensive lines of the adjoining 7th Armoured Division.

The 2nd Armoured Division, part of the Ninth Army, was 70 miles away in Germany when the Battle of the Bulge began. It was ordered to race to the scene and at the same time transferred to the First Army on 22 December 1944. It began a counter-attack on elements of two German panzer divisions on the northern flank of their penetration at the small Belgian town of Celles on Christmas Day. Once the town was secured, the division fought off several enemy counter-attacks and seized much of the surrounding countryside.

CCB of the 3rd Armoured Division brought to a halt the deepest penetration by the Sixth Panzer Army by stopping the 1st SS Panzer Division at the town of La Gleize on 20 December 1944. The combined actions of two US Army armoured divisions stopped the German Army's penetration into Belgium on the northern flank of their offensive.

The US Army Counter-Attacks

By 3 January 1945 the German counter-offensive was at an end and German forces had switched to a defensive posture. The 2nd and 3rd Armoured Divisions quickly went on the offensive against the now spent German forces in the northern part of their penetration. It would take them fourteen days to link up with Patton's Third Army coming up from the southern portion of the German penetration into Belgium.

Patton's Third Army attack to relieve the US Army units, surrounded at the Belgian crossroad town of Bastogne, began on 22 December 1944. It was spearheaded by elements of the 4th Armoured Division, which while encountering stiff German resistance pushed forward through 100 miles of ice and snow-covered terrain, reaching the town on 26 December 1944. The Germans quickly mounted a series of counter-attacks to cut through the 4th Armoured Division's route to Bastogne with no success.

Shortly after the CCR of the 4th Armoured Division broke through the German cordon, Patton wrote to the divisional commander, Gaffey:

> The outstanding celerity of your movement and the unremitting, vicious, and skillful manner in which you pushed the attack terminating at the end of four days and four nights of incessant battle in the relief of Bastogne constitute one of the finest chapters in the glorious history of the United States Army.

Patton also wrote to his wife in another bit of hyperbole that the relief of Bastogne is 'the most brilliant operation we have thus far performed and is in my opinion the outstanding achievement of this war.'

As soon as the 4th Armoured Division had broken through the siege of Bastogne, Patton began feeding in his other armoured divisions, such as the 6th and 9th, to expand the salient around the town. On 31 December 1944 Eisenhower had the 9th Armoured Division returned to Supreme Headquarters Allied Expeditionary Force (SHAEF) reserve and replaced by an infantry division. The 10th Armoured Division had entered into combat on 2 November 1944 as part of Patton's Third Army. It had fought alongside the 4th and 6th Armoured Divisions during the Lorraine campaign. It was commanded by Major General William H.H. Morris, Jr.

The 11th Armoured Division was assigned to the Third Army on 23 December 1944 and would remain with it to the conclusion of the war in the ETO. At the time, it was commanded by Major General Charles S. Kilburn. On 16 January 1945, the 11th Armoured Division coming up from the south would link up with the 2nd Armoured Division coming down from the north at the Belgian town of Houffalize and end the Bastogne operation. By 28 January 1945 the American First and Third armies reached the German frontier and re-established the lines that existed prior to the Battle of the Bulge.

The Fighting Goes On

With the end of the Battle of the Bulge the final chapter of the war in the ETO was nearing its conclusion. As the various US armies pressed forward into Germany at the start of 1945 there were a couple of occasions on which its armoured divisions demonstrated what had been learned and what had not. During the fighting in north-east France between 31 December 1944 and 25 January 1945, referred to by the Germans as Operation NORDWIND, the 14th Armoured Division, which had entered into combat in the ETO on 14 November 1944, played a part.

Unfortunately, the 14th Armoured Division, part of the Seventh Army and under the command of Major General Albert C. Smith, failed to adhere to what other more experienced armoured divisions had already mastered and in fact had already been identified as a serious problem as early as the 1940–41 war games conducted in the United States. This is seen in an extract from a post-war US Army report titled 'The Battle of Hatten-Rittershoffen: 14th Armored Division 12–20 January 1945':

> Nowhere in this action does there appear a really coordinated effort by the entire division. If there is one lesson that reverberates through and through this entire operation, it is the ghastliness of piecemeal commitment. It is truly a futile effort. Even in the main attack of January 12 [1945], CCA was committed three and one-half hours before CCB, less than a mile to the north … the division employed less than one-half of its total available combat strength in the forward echelon in the initial attack.

A more positive US Army armoured division action was performed by the 9th Armoured Division, under the command of Major General John W. Leonard. This is seen in the following extract from a post-war US Army report titled 'The 9th Armored Division in the Exploitation of Remagen Bridgehead', which took place between 28 March and 18 April 1945 and resulted in the eventual encirclement of the German city of Leipzig:

> The 9th moved so fast that in every letter received from company grade officers, their only complaint was, 'We were pushed too hard.' At times, all three

[combat] commands attacked abreast, each command having two to three columns. Resistance was either by-passed or overrun until the objectives were attained. Secondary roads and even trails were used to by-pass [enemy resistance]. Engineers and artillery were well forward in the columns. If one [combat] command was held up, the other sped on, thus causing resistance to collapse. Attacks from march column with single and double envelopment were routine, such as 70 miles in eleven hours and 68 miles in sixteen hours were commonplace. Speed was the essence.

End of the War Thoughts on Armoured Divisions

In the immediate aftermath of the Second World War, the US Army convened to identify and document what had been learned about their participation in the conflict. It would issue a number of reports, one titled 'Organization, Equipment and Tactical Employment of the Armored Division'. The report concluded that the 1943 armoured division TO&E, implemented by McNair, was a serious mistake. Rather, it suggested that in the future US Army armoured divisions should be based on a modified version of the 1942 armoured division TO&E.

In the years that followed, additional studies pushed the US Army to reorganize its immediate post-war armoured division TO&E to resemble the original 1940 TO&E. This resulted in the US Army's only remaining Second World War armoured division, the 2nd, increasing in size to 16,000 men with an authorized TO&E of 373 tanks. The 2nd Armoured Division would be joined by the reactivated 3rd Armoured Division in 1947.

With the outbreak of the Korean War in June 1950, an additional four wartime armoured divisions were reactivated. These included the 1st, 5th, 6th and 7th. The only remaining US Army armoured division today is the 1st and that is in name only as brigade combat teams (BCTs), beginning in 2006, are now the fighting elements of the modern US Army.

(**Opposite, above**) In early 1943, the Ordnance Department began a programme to upgrade its inventory of M4 series Medium Tanks based on combat experience; these would include early-production units, new production units and those already sent overseas. One of the upgrades, seen here, was the addition of 1.5in-thick armour plates welded to the pronounced driver and bow-gunner hatch hoods on M4 welded-hull medium tanks to increase protection. *(Pierre-Olivier Buan)*

(**Opposite, below**) Another important battlefield lesson learned by the Ordnance Department was the fact that the armour on both sides of the hull of the M4 series of medium tanks was too thin, as it was on the front right-hand side of the turret. The short-term solution to these issues was the welding-on of 1in-thick armour steel plates as seen here over those respective weak spots. *(Pierre-Olivier Buan)*

MORTS POUR LA LIBERATION
DE LA VALETTE DU VAR
DU 21 AU 23 AOUT 1944
CHAR VERDUN
MAIRESSE LEBRON
RENE BARREY
POLLET
ROGER SAULAS
CHAR ARTOIS
ROGER GORINI
CHAR AQUITAINE
RENE GONIN
VALBROS
MF4232
VERDUN

USA 3051632

(**Above**) In spite of the hatch hoods on the cast-armour hull M4A1 Medium Tanks being far less pronounced than those on the welded-hull M4 series Medium Tanks, in some cases the former had the 1.5in-thick welded-armour plates added anyway as seen in this photograph. This particular M4A1 tank has the early-production Combination Gun Mount M34. *(Pierre-Olivier Buan)*

(**Opposite, above**) The first armoured division to arrive in Normandy, France, was the 2nd Armoured Division, arriving on 9 June 1944. Its medium tank inventory consisted of the welded-armoured hull M4 as seen here and the cast-armour hull M4A1 tank. Both were armed with a 75mm main gun. Post-war testing of welded-armour hull and cast-armour hull M4 series Medium Tanks showed that the former offered a superior level of ballistic protection. *(Pierre-Olivier Buan)*

(**Opposite, below**) In this picture, we see the driver's position in the front hull compartment of an M4A1 Medium Tank. Located on the horizontal platform to the right of the driver's position is the foul-weather cover that could be erected over the open hatch by the driver when conditions warranted. Seen in front of the driver's seat are his two steering laterals. *(Author's collection)*

423 BGS 69

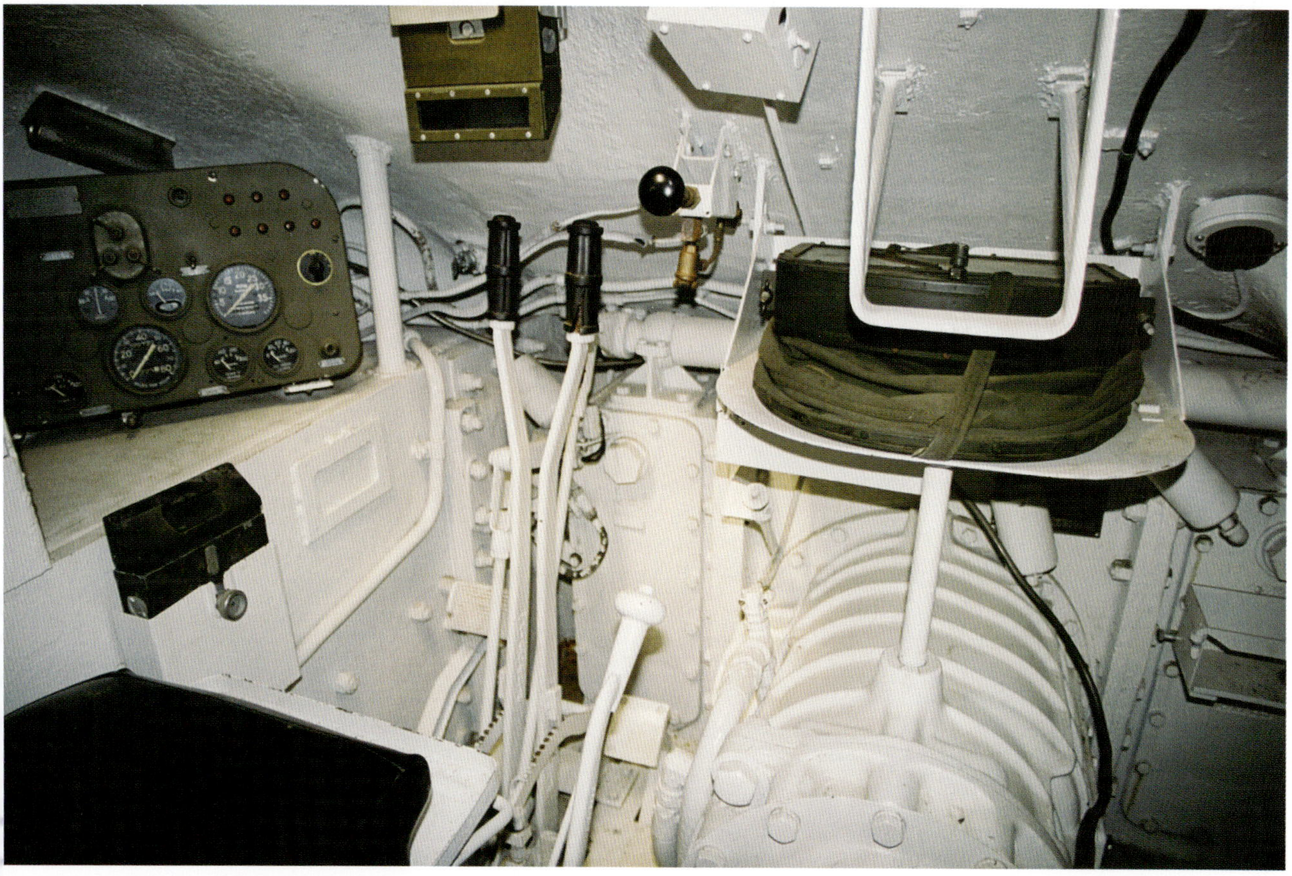

The most common protection upgrade made to the M4 Medium Tank series in the ETO was the addition of sandbags. Its effectiveness against kinetic-energy (KE) armour-piercing projectiles was almost nil but it offered some protection from shaped-charged rocket warheads. Pictured here is an M4A1 Medium Tank. *(Pierre-Olivier Buan)*

On the chest of the tanker pictured here is the black plastic SW-141 throat microphone unit. Upon entering his tank, he would use a plug to connect to the vehicle's onboard communication system. Pressing a switch on the SW-141 activated the two throat microphone elements on either side of his cartilage (Adam's apple), allowing him to communicate with other members of his crew. *(Patton Museum)*

The 4th Armoured Division first arrived in Normandy, France, on 13 July 1944. It had trained on M4A3 Medium Tanks in the United States. However, on arrival in England it was equipped with both the M4 and M4A1 Medium Tanks. Very late-production M4A1 Medium Tanks had their hull armour casting made thicker so the 1in steel welded-on armour plates as seen on this particular vehicle were no longer necessary. *(Michel Krauss)*

There were no organic quartermaster truck companies in the 1943 armoured division TO&E. Nevertheless, at least two were typically semi-permanently attached. The responsibility of moving fuel and other petroleum products from the rear echelon to the front line was assigned to the division train. Pictured here is a simulated wartime refuelling location staged at an historical military vehicle rally. *(Christophe Vallier)*

Tankers are shown both reloading their vehicle with 75mm main gun rounds and at the same time using a 5.3-gallon jerrycan to refuel their M4 series Medium Tank. The division trains of both the 1942 and 1943 armoured division TO&Es (except the medical battalion) were armed with small-arms and anti-tank rocket-launchers (bazookas) for self-protection. *(National Archives)*

(**Opposite, above**) The armoured division train, which brought ammunition and fuel to the forward echelon by truck as pictured, typically travelled at night in a number of different columns, with the order of march and its composition varying according to the tactical situation. The division train commander could request additional protection from the division's combat elements when required. *(National Archives)*

(**Opposite, below**) Located in a rear area depot in France is a large mountain of tyres needed to keep the US Army's wheeled vehicles operational in the ETO. The success of Operation COBRA in July 1944 and the subsequent dash across France by the US Army's armoured divisions through to August 1944 stretched the Allied logistical system to breaking-point as it was not prepared for that eventuality. *(National Archives)*

FIRE LADY
F-12
9△89R
F-12

(**Opposite, above**) On the lower front hull of this M5A1 Light Tank we can see a reproduction of the ad hoc hedgerow-cutter developed in July 1944 to deal with the hedgerows in Normandy, France. Tanks so equipped were sometimes nicknamed 'rhino tanks' due to their appearance. Their actual contribution to the eventual success of the First Army armoured divisions' fighting in the hedgerows of Normandy is more myth than reality. *(Christophe Vallier)*

(**Above**) As unarmoured commercial bulldozers proved too vulnerable in front-line service in armoured divisions, the corps of engineers developed and fielded the Bulldozer, Tank Mounting, M1 beginning in the latter half of 1943. It is seen here attached to an M4A1 Medium Tank. The bulldozer blade was attached to side arms on either side of the tank that pivoted from the centre bogie wheel assemblies. *(Patton Museum)*

(**Opposite, below**) Pictured here is an M32B2 Tank Recovery Vehicle based on an M4A1 Medium Tank. In a post-war Armour School report comes this comment: 'The M32 series tank retriever has such obvious limitations as a recovery vehicle that it seems unnecessary to mention more than two of the most serious limitations: (1) the narrow tracks prohibit its use in soft terrain; and (2) the open turret prohibits the use of the vehicle under fire.' *(Patton Museum)*

T271199

U.S.A.
3045638-S
SUZIE
D-10

(**Opposite, above**) Despite the poor showing of the US Army's light tanks during the fighting in Tunisia, the armoured divisions that went ashore in France during the summer and autumn of 1944 seemed unaware of the lessons already learned and made extensive use of the M5A1 Light Tank, an example of which is seen here. The results were predictable, with extremely high losses until they were eventually restricted to secondary roles. *(Andreas Kirchhoff)*

(**Opposite, below**) According to an October 1944 report by a tank battalion in the ETO, the welding of an extra armour plate just under the driver and bow-gunner positions on light tanks dramatically cut down on losses. The US Army lost a total of 777 M5A1 Light Tanks in combat in the ETO and another 424 in the Italian theatre. Pictured here at an historical military rally is an M5A1 Light Tank. *(Author's collection)*

(**Above**) The high losses of M5A1 Light Tanks in the ETO prompted the Armoured Section of the 12th Army Group in the ETO to request in September 1944 their replacement as soon as possible with the M24 Light Tank seen here. Within armoured divisions the first elements to receive them were the reconnaissance squadrons and not the tank companies. *(Pierre-Olivier Buan)*

Infantrymen on the rear engine deck of an M8 Light Armoured Car are prepared for the worst as they enter a burning town. Of the fifteen armoured divisions that served in the ETO, it was the 8th that spent the most days in combat at 260. The highest loss rate was incurred by the 3rd Armoured Division with 2,540 killed and 7,331 wounded during 231 days of combat. *(Patton Museum)*

(**Opposite, above**) Pictured here is an earlier-production or first-generation M4A3 Medium Tank with the very pronounced driver and bow-gunner hatch protrusions on the upper front hull. The reason for this design arrangement, which resulted in very small and narrow overhead hatches for the driver and bow-gunner, was the 57-degree slope on the vehicle's upper front hull. *(Pierre-Olivier Buan)*

(**Opposite, below**) To eliminate the protruding hatch hoods for the driver and bow-gunner on the first-generation M4A3 Medium Tank, the second-generation M4A3 Medium Tank had the upper front hull plate as seen here reset at an angle of only 47 degrees. This allowed for the addition of larger angled and counter-balanced overhead hatches for the driver and bow-gunner. *(Pierre-Olivier Buan)*

3△32△
C 5

46

(**Above**) There are two key identifying features for both first-generation and second-generation M4A3 Medium Tanks, which can be seen on the vehicle pictured here. First was the steep sloped angle of the rear hull plate, and second the horizontal multi-slotted exhaust deflector located at the very bottom of the tank pictured. The exhaust deflector could be raised for access to rear engine access doors. *(Chun-lun Hsu)*

(**Opposite, above**) A major design feature of the second-generation M4A3 Medium Tank besides the reset of the upper front hull was a new main gun ammunition storage system. This involved relocating the majority of main gun rounds from the upper hull sides to the bottom of the tank's hull in racks surrounded by a liquid referred to as 'Ammudamp'. M4 series Medium Tanks so equipped had the word 'Wet' added to their vehicle data plates. *(Pierre-Olivier Buan)*

(**Opposite, below**) The development of the 'Wet' ammunition storage system on the second-generation M4A3 Medium Tank, designated the M4A3(75) Wet seen here, was to improve the chances for the crew to exit the tank before its onboard main gun ammunition caught fire and/or detonated. However, its actual wartime effectiveness proved minimal as it did not quench the main gun ammunition fires on board tanks so fitted. *(Pierre-Olivier Buan)*

5A 760Д

USA 3019428

USA
3083084
FOR SHIPMENT
AA00 R-ORD II SF36 CP47

(**Opposite, above**) In this image we see a second-generation dozer-equipped M4A3 Medium Tank armed with a 105mm howitzer, resulting in the designation M4A3(105). Spotting features for the vehicle include the thicker main gun barrel and a different design of the full-width cast-armour gun shield. This vehicle and its counterpart the M4(105) had authorized storage for sixty-eight main gun rounds. *(Mathieu George)*

(**Above**) As a stopgap until the M26 Heavy Tank could be fielded in the ETO, a decision was made to dramatically up-armour the hulls of 254 brand-new M4A3(75) Wet Medium Tanks coming off the assembly lines combined with a new thickly-armoured turret. The Ordnance Committee designated the modified tank the Assault Tank M4A3E2 in March 1944, an example of which is seen here. *(Pierre-Olivier Buan)*

(**Opposite, below**) The initial units of the Assault Tank M4A3E2 arrived in the ETO in late 1944. The example pictured here belonged to the 4th Armoured Division and was nicknamed 'Cobra King'. It was the first tank of the division to break through German lines on 26 December 1944 and drive into Bastogne, Belgium, thereby relieving the siege of the 101st Airborne Division. *(Don Moriarty)*

(**Above**) The fielding of a second generation of M4 series Medium Tanks armed with a 76mm main gun came about when the senior leadership of the Armoured Force was convinced by the British that the German Army would soon be fielding new tanks that would have armour impervious to the 75mm main guns on first-generation M4 series Medium Tanks. Pictured here is an M4A1(76) Wet, which first entered combat in the ETO in July 1944. *(Pierre-Olivier Buan)*

(**Opposite, above**) Besides producing a second-generation M4A1 Medium Tank armed with a 76mm main gun and other improvements, which was designated the M4A1(76) Wet, the preferred first-generation M4A3 Medium Tank was also redesigned to produce a second-generation model seen here that was designated the M4A3(76) Wet. It first entered combat in the ETO in October 1944. *(Patton Museum)*

(**Opposite, below**) The vertical volute spring suspension (VVSS) system combined with 16.56in tracks of the first-generation of M4 series Medium Tanks was not the optimum choice, but it was what was available at the time. Beginning in early 1941, the Ordnance Department began work on what eventually became the horizontal volute spring suspension (HVSS) system that rode on 23in-wide tracks. An example of that is seen on this M4A3(76) Wet. *(Author's collection)*

U.S.A.
30100252

M4A3E8
1944

Production of the M4A3(76) Wet seen here with the HVSS began in August 1944. The new suspension system increased the tank's weight by between 3,000 to 5,000lb depending on the type of track used. It also increased the width of tanks so fitted up to 9.8ft when fitted with sand shields. By contrast, the width of first-generation M4 series Medium Tanks without sand shields was 8.7ft. *(Author's collection)*

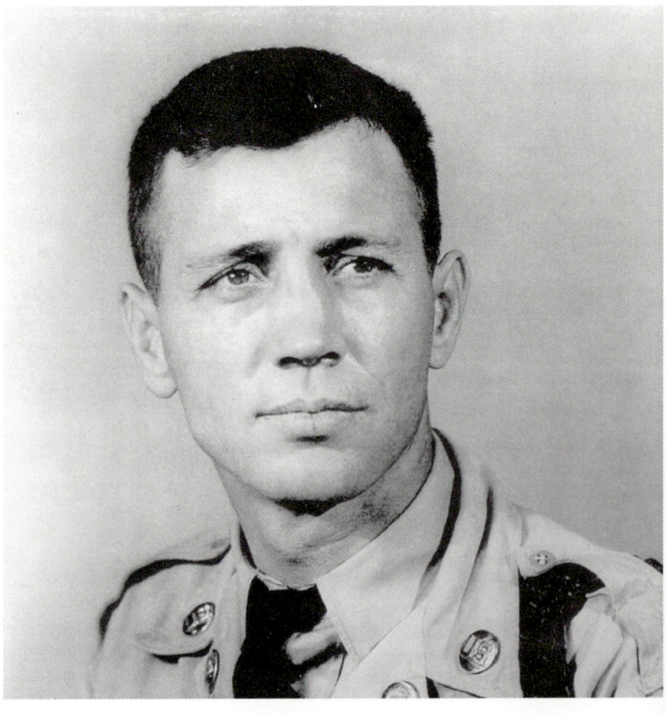

Pictured here is Lafayette G. Pool who was the US Army's most famous tanker from the Second World War. Serving with the 3rd Armoured Division from June to September 1944 in the ETO, Pool is credited with 12 enemy tanks destroyed, 258 other types of armoured fighting vehicles (AFVs) destroyed, with 250 enemy personnel taken prisoner and another 1,000 killed. In the process, he lost three M4 series Medium Tanks, the second and third armed with the 76mm main gun. *(Patton Museum)*

Production of the muzzle brake seen on the M4A3(76) Wet Medium Tank pictured here began in July 1944. It was in response to the problem of too much dust and debris being kicked up by non-muzzle-brake-equipped 76mm main guns. As production of the muzzle brakes lagged behind that of the four versions of the 76mm gun, the last three models had the ends of their barrels threaded to accept muzzle brakes when available. *(Chris Hughes)*

The M4A1(76) Wet with 23in tracks (HVSS) began arriving in the ETO in the spring of 1945. This particular vehicle is a post-war remanufactured unit supplied to the French Army under a military assistance programme (MAP). There has been some question as to whether the M4A1(76) Wet with HVSS ever saw combat with the US Army in the ETO; however, a signal corps photograph dated 20 April 1945 confirms at least one was in service in Germany on that date. *(Pierre-Olivier Buan)*

GUN - PARTS
BOLT & TOOL
CAL. 30
BARRELS

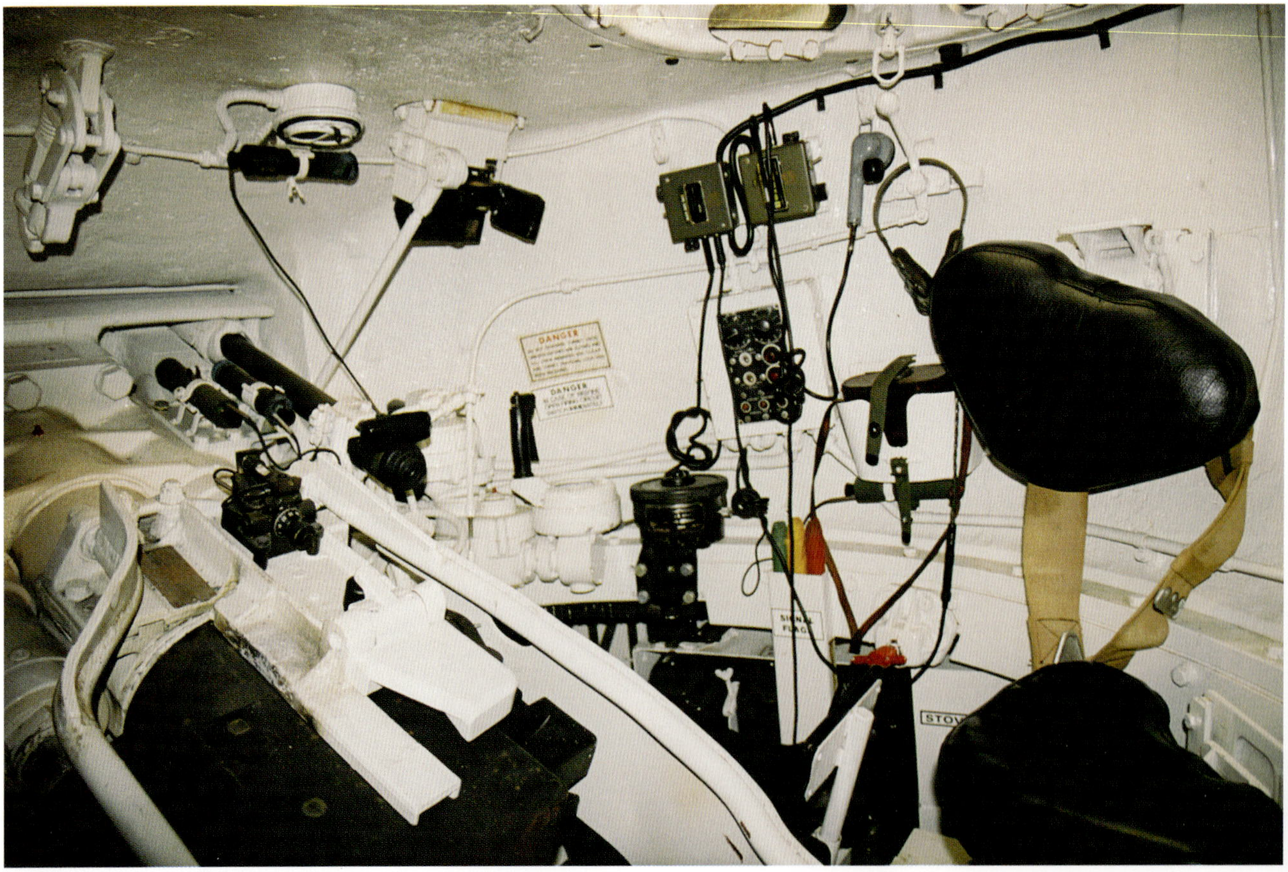
DANGER
DANGER

(**Opposite, above**) Pictured inside an M4A3(76) Wet with HVSS is the bow-gunner's position. Below his seat was an escape hatch and behind his seat a main gun ammunition storage container that held thirty rounds. As the .30 calibre machine gun had no optical sight, aiming the weapon involved the bow-gunner watching the tracers through his overhead hatch periscope. *(Author's collection)*

(**Opposite, below**) Taken from the loader's side of an M4A3(76) Wet with HVSS is this view of the tank commander's position. Visible are his two seats, with the bottom one used when buttoned-up and the higher second seat employed when he had his overhead hatch open and wished to look out over the top of the tank. Also seen are the gunner's optical sight and some of the gun controls. *(Author's collection)*

(**Above**) Early on in the ETO, armour-piercing (AP) rounds fired from high-velocity guns accounted for 50 per cent of US Army tank losses. However, by the autumn of 1944, the proportion of tank losses due to shaped-charge warheads increased from 10 per cent to 35 per cent. In response, some tank crews began adding ever-increasing numbers of sandbags to their vehicles as seen here. *(Patton Museum)*

(**Opposite, above**) Lacking enough of the M4A3E2 Assault Tanks in the Third Army, its commander, Patton, ordered that all M4A3(76) Wet Medium Tanks riding on HVSS be up-armoured with the cut-out armour from destroyed American or German tanks. An example of the end result is seen on the tank pictured here, with add-on armour having been applied to both its hull and turret. *(Tank Museum)*

(**Opposite, below**) The crews of cast-armoured-hull medium tanks, such as the M4A1(76) Wet pictured here, obviously believed there was no reason why they could not add improvised steel armour kits to their vehicles. They therefore managed to jury-rig a support system for adding a flat armour plate to the rounded front hull contours of their tank. This M4A1(76) Wet is riding on the original VVSS system. *(Patton Museum)*

(**Above**) Another method by which US Army tank crews in the ETO sought a bit more protection from enemy weapons was the addition of cement with reinforcing bars on the front upper hulls of their tanks as seen here on an M4A3(75) Wet. Visible are the wooden beams that held in the cement as it dried. Note the infantrymen on the rear deck of the vehicle. *(National Archives)*

4215753-S
HQ-58
MILITARY POLICE

The signal corps caption states that the young soldier of the 3rd Armoured Division pictured here is receiving fire instructions via a radio-telephone for his howitzer. Note the submachine gun stored in the half-track. He wears what was called the 'tanker's jacket', which had knitted wrists, collar and waistband. It was made of weatherproofed cotton, with a blanket liner. *(National Archives)*

(**Opposite, above**) Within the 1943 armoured division TO&E was a Military Police platoon. It was attached to the headquarters company of the division train and was commanded by the division's provost marshal. It performed a wide variety of roles including traffic control and the handling of prisoners of war (PoWs). In this picture, we see Military Police Jeeps following a truck carrying German PoWs. *(National Archives)*

(**Opposite, below**) The M7 series of Howitzer Motor Carriages (HMCs) were not equipped with radios as were all tanks. Rather, when in battery firing position, they received their fire orders via field telephones as is evident in this picture. There were six M7s in each armoured field artillery battery, with a total of eighteen in an armoured field artillery battalion. Each battery was also equipped with seven half-tracks. *(National Archives)*

FROM U.S. PORT AGENCY
WAR SHIPPING ADM. N.Y.
GROSS WT 5375 LBS
COMBAT WT 7190 LBS
HEIGHT 81 IN
WIDTH 77 IN
LENGTH 165 IN
USMC

Pictured here is Major General John Shirley Wood, commander of the 4th Armoured Division from January to December 1944. He was nicknamed 'Tiger Jack' or 'P' Wood. The first came from his habit of nervously pacing like a caged animal. The 'P', standing for 'Professor', was a term of endearment acquired at West Point, where he spent much time tutoring his fellow cadets in their studies. *(Patton Museum)*

(**Opposite, above**) The first and second generations of M4 series Medium Tanks armed with the 75mm main gun could be employed in the indirect fire role as pictured here. This was not an optimum role for the vehicle as few tank commanders had the required training to perform the complex computations needed to be effective in the indirect artillery fire role and to factor in barrel wear. *(National Archives)*

(**Opposite, below**) Found in both the 1942 and 1943 armoured division TO&Es was the Dodge WC-56 three-quarter-ton 4 x 4 Command and Reconnaissance Truck seen here. It was the 1942 replacement for the Dodge WC-6 and WC-8 half-ton 4 x 4 Command and Reconnaissance cars. With a winch, the company designation was WC-57. It was generally intended for use by staff officers. Approximately 27,000 units were constructed. *(Chris Hughes)*

USA
40177445-S

U S ARMY 73463813

(**Opposite, above**) The Ordnance Department knew that the German Army would field more heavily-armoured tanks in the future. To prepare for this they came up with the 90mm Gun Motor Carriage (GMC) M36 seen here, which was standardized in July 1944. It consisted of the hull of the 3in Gun Motor Carriage (GMC) M10A1 with a new cast-armour open turret armed with a 90mm main gun. *(Pierre-Olivier Buan)*

(**Opposite, below**) As the supply of M10A1 hulls was exhausted by the conversion into 90mm Gun Motor Carriage (GMC) M36s, it was decided to employ the unmodified hulls of M4A3(75) Wet Medium Tanks as a platform upon which to mount the 90mm main gun-armed turret from the M36. This mating resulted in the vehicle pictured here that was labelled the 90mm Gun Motor Carriage (GMC) M36B1. *(Chris Hughes)*

(**Above**) It was not uncommon for US Army armoured divisions to have attached towed field artillery batteries when the need arose. For towing the 105mm Howitzer M1 and the 155mm Howitzer M1918 there was the unarmoured vehicle seen here labelled the 13-ton High-Speed Tractor M5. It was based on the chassis of the M3 Light Tank and had a towing capacity of up to 16,000lb. *(Author's collection)*

(**Above**) For towing artillery pieces weighing between 18,000lb and 30,000lb the US Army fielded the unarmoured vehicle seen here designated the 18-ton High Speed Tractor M4. The chassis incorporated components from both the Medium Tank M3 and M4 series, such as the tracks. Unlike the medium tanks, it had a rear trailing idler as seen on the Light Tank series M3 and M5. *(Pierre-Olivier Buan)*

(**Opposite, above**) Pictured here is an M3A1 Half-Track Personnel Carrier. The three rifle companies in each of the three armoured infantry battalions in the 1943 armoured division TO&E had twenty half-tracks. Each of the three rifle platoons in a company had five half-tracks. The anti-tank platoon of the company had three half-tracks towing the 57mm Gun M1. In the company headquarters platoon, there were two half-tracks. *(Chris Hughes)*

(**Opposite, below**) Of the five M3A1 Half-Track Personnel Carriers that made up a platoon in the rifle company of an armoured infantry battalion, three carried a squad of twelve men. Of the other two half-tracks, one carried a light machine-gun squad and the other a mortar squad armed with two 60mm mortars. The soldiers that served on these half-tracks had a couple of nicknames: 'armoured doughs' or 'blitz doughs'. *(TACOM Historical Office)*

U.S.A.
HQ 22

LEFT HAND
DRIVE
NO SIGNALS
OLD
SMOKIE!
C-4

U.S.A
40102848
MALIN
288-169

(**Opposite, above**) In German Army units equipped with their half-track counterpart to the US Army M3A1 Half-Track Personnel Carrier seen here, the armoured infantry, known as 'panzer grenadiers', generally fought from on board their vehicles. By contrast, the US Army armoured infantry was taught to dismount from their half-tracks before entering into combat. *(Christophe Vallier)*

(**Opposite, below**) To improve the off-road mobility of its first-generation M4 series Medium Tanks riding on the vertical volute spring suspension (VVSS) system, the Chrysler Corporation was tasked with the development of a spacer system that would allow extended end connectors to be fitted to both sides of a tank's tracks. An example of that arrangement is seen here, which would result in 'E9' being added to a tank's designation. *(Paul and Loren Hannah)*

(**Above**) The very high losses of M4, M4A1 and M4A3 Medium Tanks (both first- and second-generation) incurred by the US Army armoured divisions that took part in the Battle of the Bulge could not be made up immediately from existing stockpiles in the ETO. This resulted in the US Army taking into service a number of M4A2 Medium Tanks as seen here from British Army stockpiles in the ETO. *(Pierre-Olivier Buan)*

USA
3083084
FOR SHIPMENT

elm Baums

(**Opposite, above**) It took time for the US Army to grasp the requirement for a well-armed and thickly-armoured tank that could do battle on even terms with late-war German tanks and assault guns. That tank is pictured here and was standardized as the Heavy Tank M26 in March 1945. It was armed with the same 90mm main gun that was on the 90mm Gun Motor Carriage M36 and M36B1. *(Rob Cogan)*

(**Opposite, below**) Seen here in Germany in March 1945 is a Heavy Tank M26. It weighed approximately 90,000lb and was protected by up to 114mm of armour on its cast-armour gun shield. The near-vertical sides of its cast-armour turret were 76mm thick. The upper front hull was sloped at 46 degrees and was 101mm thick. Like the M4 series of medium tanks, it had a five-man crew. *(Patton Museum)*

(**Above**) Shown here is an M4A3(105) fitted with the horizontal volute spring suspension (HVSS) system. A total of 4,680 units of the 105mm-armed M4 series Medium Tanks were built between February 1944 and June 1945. Of that number, 1,641 were the M4(105) and the remaining 3,039 units the M4A3(105). Unlike the 75mm or 76mm main gun-armed versions of the M4 Medium Tank series, they lacked a turret power traverse system. *(Pierre-Olivier Buan)*

(**Above**) The success of the 155mm Gun Motor Carriage (GMC) M12 in the ETO led to development of the more capable 155mm Gun Motor Carriage (GMC) M40 seen here. Unlike the former, based on the M3 Medium Tank chassis, the latter was based on various components of the second-generation of M4 series Medium Tanks. Only a single example made it to the ETO before the fighting stopped. *(Paul and Loren Hannah)*

(**Opposite, above**) In a signal corps photograph dated 2 February 1945, two soldiers are looking at the sign put up by the 6th Armoured Division welcoming them to Germany. The 6th Armoured Division spent 231 days in combat and during that time had 1,238 men killed, another 4,246 wounded and 503 missing in action. *(National Archives)*

(**Opposite, below**) This picture nicely sums up the end of the war in Europe as long lines of German soldiers are seen marching into captivity down the median of a German *autobahn*. On either side of them pass the tanks and trucks of the 6th Armoured Division. The division lost 196 medium tanks and 24 light tanks during its time in combat. It was credited with capturing 61,864 prisoners by the time the fighting ceased in the ETO. *(National Archives)*

YOU ARE NOW ENTERING
GERMANY
THROUGH THE COURTESY OF THE
U S
6TH ARMORED DIVISION

Notes

Notes

Notes

Notes

Notes

Notes

Notes